THE

MUTUAL FUND KIT

▶ IDENTIFYING YOUR OBJECTIVES

▶ BUILDING YOUR PROFITABLE PORTFOLIO

▶ SELECTING THE BEST FUNDS

▶ MEASURING YOUR FUND'S PERFORMANCE

Bay Gruber

Dearborn
Financial Publishing, Inc.®

Executive Editor: Cynthia A. Zigmund
Managing Editor: Jack L. Kiburz
Interior Design: Lucy Jenkins
Cover Design: S. Laird Jenkins Corporation
Typesetting: Elizabeth Pitts

Library of Congress Cataloging-in-Publication Data

Gruber, Bay.
    The mutual fund kit / Bay Gruber.
      p. cm.
    Includes index.
    ISBN 0-7931-2492-1 (pbk.)
    1. Mutual funds. I. Title.
  HG4530.G765 1997
332.63'27–dc21   97-19758
                                         CIP

Contents

Preface

Why read a book about mutual funds? Many people believe that mutual funds are (1) easy to select for purchase and (2) don't have to be monitored the way that individual stocks and bonds do. For these two reasons, investors need a better understanding of owning mutual funds. In reality, selecting an appropriate mutual fund for your portfolio may be more complicated than purchasing an individual stock or bond. You can choose from more than 10,000 mutual funds (including the different share classes) in over 350 different mutual fund management companies. The New York Stock Exchange alone lists approximately 2,500 stocks, of which several hundred household-name companies are represented. The Nasdaq Stock Market℠ and the American Stock Exchange trade thousands of stocks as well. The number of federal government, municipal, and corporate bond issues also runs in the thousands.

Not all mutual funds are alike. Every individual mutual fund has distinct investment objectives and risks, to name just a few important differences. Also, each mutual fund has a unique portfolio of underlying securities. When you purchase a mutual fund, you are investing in the portfolio of these underlying securities. The performance of the fund's portfolio determines the performance of your mutual fund investment.

To be a more knowledgeable investor, you need to take a closer look at the fund's category, investment objectives, risk considerations, underlying securities, costs, expenses, fees, and management style. Managing your portfolio involves reviewing, selecting, purchasing, monitoring, and adjusting your mutual fund holdings based on your *investment policy statement*. The seven steps to create a viable investment policy statement are:

1. Prepare your investor's profile.
2. Understand your risks and returns.
3. Allocate your assets.
4. Select your mutual funds.
5. Measure your risks and returns.
6. Monitor your mutual funds' performance.
7. Periodically review your portfolio and investment policy statement.

Portfolio management may be as basic and simple, or as complicated and sophisticated, as you want. *The Mutual Fund Kit* presents some of the traditional portfolio management and modern portfolio theory terms. This book also focuses on comparing your fund's performance to an appropriate return or benchmark, such as your investment objective, an absolute number, a "risk-free" investment, a corresponding mutual fund index, and a corresponding market average or index. Asset allocation and diversification are cornerstones of investing and are discussed extensively in this book. Costs, expenses, and fees associated with buying, selling, and holding shares of mutual funds also are discussed.

From numerous consultations with my clients over the past 25 years, I have come to believe that educating you, the investor, is paramount for your success in becoming financially secure. *The Mutual Fund Kit* provides you with a framework to understand the mechanics of mutual funds, asset allocation, diversification, and how to prepare your investment policy statement.

However, *The Mutual Fund Kit* is not meant to be a complete financial plan or comprehensive investment portfolio program. Investing in mutual funds is only one alternative for investing in money market securities, bonds, and stocks. In many cases, purchasing individual securities or using other investing methods may be more suitable or profitable than investing in mutual funds. Of course, other methods of investing also carry the same and sometimes additional risks as those associated with investing in mutual funds. Investment objectives of mutual funds are not guaranteed and are only an objective of the funds.

I wrote *The Mutual Fund Kit* and obtained the information and data from sources considered reliable; their accuracy or completeness is not guaranteed, however. Individuals should consult their personal tax or legal advisers before making any tax or legal investment decision.

Acknowledgments

With assistance from other people this book became a better educational tool for you. Special gratitude goes to Elizabeth A. Vetell for her support, significant insights, and beneficial comments. Deep appreciation is given to June A. Newell for her outstanding assistance and excellent editing of the manuscript. Also, thanks are extended to A. James Bach, Michael Hanley, Richard A. Welch, and to many other people for their contributions.

Sincere recognition goes to my associates, Renn G. Gruber, Judith K. Joyce, Cynthia M. Krupo, and Marie F. Somers, who encouraged me while writing this book.

Compliments to Jack Kiburz, Cynthia A. Zigmund, Ro Sila, and Elizabeth Pitts for their superb assistance and foresight during the publishing process.

CHAPTER 1

An Introduction to Mutual Funds

Investors buy billions of dollars worth of mutual funds each year. Most investors hold some mutual funds in their personal portfolios, individual retirement accounts (IRAs), simplified employee plans (SEPs), 401(k) plans, 403(b) plans, and other pension and profit-sharing plans. Many investors depend on the returns from their mutual funds for retirement and financial security. Understanding what a mutual fund is and how it operates will make you a more informed investor when purchasing mutual funds for or selling mutual funds from your portfolio.

Many people call buying mutual funds an "easy" method of investing because they do not have to choose each investment, follow its performance, decide when to buy and sell, figure commissions, or perform any of the other services the mutual fund management does for its clients. However, mutual funds come in many shapes and sizes. Mutual funds differ from other investments based on organizational structure, regulation, portfolio management, stated investment objective, risk, investment characteristics, management fees, expenses, sales charges, and 12b-1 distribution fees.

How This Book Is Organized

This chapter will give you an overview of mutual funds—their structure, financial terms you will need to know, what to expect and what not to expect from your investment, etc. Once you understand the basics, the following chapters will give detailed information on each aspect of mutual fund investing so you can build the best portfolio to meet your investment objectives.

Classification of Investment Companies

The Investment Company Act of 1940 provides for the registration and regulation of the operations and management of investment companies. To do business under the laws of the United States, investment companies must register with the Securities and Exchange Commission (SEC). An investment company invests, reinvests, owns, holds, or trades securities. Investment companies fall into three principle classes:

1. Face-amount certificate company
2. Unit investment trust
3. Management company

A *face-amount certificate* company is an investment company that issues face-amount certificates of the installment type. A *unit investment trust* is an investment company organized under a trust indenture, without a board of directors, that issues only redeemable securities, each of which represents an undivided interest in a unit of specified securities such as stocks or bonds. A *management company* is any investment company that is not a face-amount certificate company or a unit investment trust.

Management companies are divided into *open-end* and *closed-end companies*. An open-end company means a management company that is offering for sale or has outstanding any redeemable security of which it is the issuer. An *open-end fund* is commonly called a *mutual fund*. The primary difference between a closed-end fund and an open-end fund is that the closed-end fund issues a fixed number of shares and the open-end fund issues new shares on a continual basis. After the initial offering by a closed-end fund, the shares are typically traded (bought and sold) on an exchange, such as the New York Stock Exchange, among investors. After the initial offering of an open-end fund, the fund sells new shares and buys back (redeems) existing shares. Shares in an open-end fund are only purchased from and redeemed to the issuing management company. ***Only registered, open-end management investment companies (mutual funds) are discussed in this book.***

Diversified and Nondiversified Funds

Mutual funds are divided into diversified and nondiversified funds. A *diversified fund* meets the following requirements as defined by the Investment Company Act of 1940: "At least 75 percent of the value of its total assets is represented by cash, Government securities, securities of other investment companies, and other securities for the purpose of this calculation limited in respect of any issuer to an amount not greater in value than 5 percent of the value of the total assets of such management company and to not more than 10 percent of the outstanding voting securities of such issuer."

A *nondiversified fund* does not have to meet the above requirements and may, therefore, invest a greater portion of its assets in the securities of a single issuer; thus it is subject to greater exposure of risk (see Chapter 3 for more about risks and returns).

Regulated Investment Companies

Both a diversified and nondiversified company can qualify as a regulated investment company (RIC) under the federal income tax laws, and then are subject to the applicable diversification requirements of the Internal Revenue Code.

The benefit of being classified as a regulated investment company is that the fund is not taxed on its income and capital gains. This provision protects the shareholder from the possibility of double taxation. *Double taxation* occurs when the fund is taxed on its earnings and then distributes the after-tax earnings to shareholders who are then taxed again on the distribution.

For an investment company to qualify as a regulated investment company, it must register under the Investment Company Act of

1940 and meet the following five Internal Revenue Code subchapter M requirements:

1. At least 90 percent of investment company taxable income (including net short-term capital gains, if any) and net tax-exempt income for the taxable year is distributed.
2. At least 90 percent of its gross income is from dividends, interest, and capital gains from sales of the RIC's held securities.
3. Less than 30 percent of the fund's gross income is derived from gains on sales or other dispositions of securities held for less than three months.
4. The company may not have invested more than 25 percent of its total assets in the securities of any one issuer or of two or more issuers in the same industry.
5. In relation to 50 percent of its total assets, more than 5 percent of its total assets are invested in the securities of a single issuer, or more than 10 percent of the voting securities of any issuer, as of the end of its fiscal quarters.

Trusts and Corporations

An investment company (an open-end management company) is organized either as a corporation or a trust (commonly called a Massachusetts business trust). Therefore, the mutual fund has either a board of directors or trustees, respectively.

Your Mutual Fund Investment and Who Manages It

Understanding your mutual fund and who manages it are valuable information for you. The prospectus explains, among other items, who is the investment manager, factors that may affect the fund's performance, type of fund, and underlying securities that may be purchased. Review these items carefully so you know what type of investment you are making.

The Prospectus

Read the prospectus carefully before investing. The Securities Act of 1933 requires each fund to issue a prospectus (information publication) that describes that fund's securities being offered for sale to the public. Like a blueprint, the prospectus tells you everything about the fund, such as investment objective(s), risk considerations, investment manager, portfolio manager, securities the fund can purchase, investment restrictions, sales charges, management fees, expenses, 12b-1 distribution fees, procedures for purchasing and redeeming (selling) shares, shareholder services, dividend and distribution policies, and past performance. One item the prospectus *cannot* tell you is the fund's future performance. A prospectus is usually updated once a year. Request and read a fund's current prospectus before you make the decision on whether to invest in that fund.

Each fund's portfolio manager may invest only in the securities described in the prospectus. Depending on and limited by the investment objective(s) and fund policies, the fund may buy U.S. Treasury, federal agency, corporate, and municipal notes and bonds; certificates of deposit (CDs); domestic or foreign stocks and bonds; and other marketable securities.

Investment Manager and Portfolio Manager

Typically, the mutual fund's investment manager or adviser is a firm (management company); the portfolio manager is an individual. The management company offers a variety of funds called a *family of funds* or a *fund complex.* The company buys and sells the securities for all these funds and performs other tasks listed later in this chapter under shareholder services. The portfolio manager, on the other hand, makes the trading decisions for a particular fund, restricted by that fund's investment objective(s) as defined in its prospectus.

Net Asset Value (NAV)

The fund's *net asset value* (NAV) is its current per-share selling price. The NAV fluctuates, based on the performance of the securities held in the fund. As stated in the prospectus, you may purchase shares from the fund and redeem (sell) shares back to the fund any business day. A business day is any day the New York Stock Exchange is open.

Therefore, you buy or redeem shares at the current net asset value. Funds are listed in newspapers' financial pages under either "mutual funds" or "investment companies" and the NAV is listed for each.

Factors Affecting Share Prices of Mutual Funds

The net asset value of a mutual fund is affected by the prices of the underlying securities. Some of the factors that affect those securities are:

- Economic conditions, both domestic and foreign
- Strength or weakness of the securities markets
- Interest rate changes
- Profitability of the companies whose shares are held in the fund's portfolio
- Changes in the credit ratings of the bonds in the fund's portfolio
- Confidence in the market
- Foreign currency exchange rates (if applicable)
- Other factors

After expenses, a mutual fund pays shareholders the net investment income in the form of *dividends.* A mutual fund earns income when the fund receives dividends and interest from the portfolio's securities. It also earns capital gains when the fund sells the portfolio's securities at a net profit. A mutual fund pays shareholders the net realized capital gains (profits from securities sold at a profit minus losses from securities sold at a loss) in the form of *capital gains distributions.*

Types of Funds

The fund's investment objective(s) is your key to selecting suitable funds for your portfolio. The fund's name often tells you the type of fund it is; however, the name cannot tell everything about the fund's investment objective(s) or the risks involved in investing in that fund. Several major types of mutual funds are:

- Money market funds
- Stock funds
- Bond funds
- Balanced funds
- Asset allocation funds

You may want to diversify your assets by spreading your investment dollars among several types of mutual funds. Chapter 11 will discuss diversifying your investments.

Mutual funds are normally categorized by investment objective(s) of the fund. Some of the more common categories are:

- Preservation of capital
- Aggressive growth
- Growth
- Growth and income
- Equity income
- Total return
- Taxable income
- Tax-exempt income
- High yield (also known as high income)

Another method for categorizing a mutual fund is by the type of underlying securities in it. Some categories are:

- Money market securities
- Large-capitalization stock
- Mid-capitalization stock
- Small-capitalization stock
- Utility stock
- International stock
- Corporate bond
- Government bond
- Municipal bond
- International bond

How funds are categorized and how each category may fit in your investment strategy will be discussed in detail in the following chapters.

Underlying Securities in Mutual Fund Portfolios

You must understand the underlying securities held in a mutual fund or you will not know what you are investing in or what risks you are exposed to. As mentioned above, each mutual fund has an investment objective to which the portfolio manager must adhere. The portfolio manager must buy securities for the mutual fund that he or she believes will meet its investment objective. Therefore, when you are buying a mutual fund, you are investing in the securities that the portfolio manager in turn bought for the mutual fund. The performance and characteristics of the underlying securities in the mutual fund will determine the risks, income, capital appreciation, taxation, and expected overall return to you.

Your own investment objective should be compatible with the mutual fund's investment objective. However, the better way of looking at the mutual fund's investment objective is to determine if you are willing to own the individual underlying securities. Owning shares in the mutual fund is the same as if you purchased those individual securities.

Chapters 12, 13, and 14 discuss the investment characteristics of stocks, bonds, and money market securities. You may want to read additional investment books for more detailed explanations so you can discuss them with your investment professional.

Costs of Buying and Selling Mutual Funds

In the prospectus, you will find listed the fund's total expenses including any and all sales charges, redemption fees, 12b-1 fees, exchange fees, and other expenses. Mutual fund management companies must pass along the costs of doing business—overhead, salaries, etc.—to investors. Such charges are usually described by how they are applied to the purchase or sale of mutual fund shares:

- Front-end sales charge (FESC)
- Contingent deferred sales charge (CDSC)
- Level-load (LL)
- No-load (NL)

See Chapter 5 for detailed explanations of these charges.

Annual Operating Expenses

Every fund, whether it is FESC, CDSC, LL, or NL, pays a *management fee* to the investment company for the advice on and administration of the fund's assets. Also, each fund has "other expenses," such as valuating the fund's securities, operating the fund, safekeeping the securities, and hiring transfer agents and independent accountants.

Another annual expense may be the *12b-1 distribution fee,* also known as the *12b-1 fee,* that covers the fund's selling costs and service fee for maintaining shareholder accounts, and for whatever shareholder services may be offered by that fund.

Benefits of Mutual Funds

You can enjoy many benefits by investing in mutual funds, such as: pursue an investment objective(s), earn income, enjoy professional portfolio management, have a diversified portfolio, gain access to foreign markets, take advantage of dividend reinvestment, and buy and sell shares easily.

Investment objectives. Each mutual fund prospectus states precisely the fund's investment objectives. Knowing those objectives will help you determine if that fund is suitable for your portfolio and overall investment goal.

You may select from numerous funds whose various investment objectives may be:

- Preservation of capital
- Long-term growth
- Maximum capital appreciation
- Current income
- High current income
- Tax-exempt income
- Growth and income

A fund's investment objective is only that: an objective. The mutual fund cannot give any assurances or guarantees that the investment objective will be met. The shareholder risks his or her principal when investing in any securities, including mutual funds.

Dividend and capital gains distributions. By investing in a mutual fund, you participate in the fund's earnings and capital gains, if any. The benefit to you is that the fund can pay you the net investment income and net realized capital gains in either cash or in additional shares through its reinvestment program. By reinvesting your dividend and/or capital gains distributions, you purchase additional shares on which future dividends may be paid. Therefore, this can result in the potential benefit of compounding returns over time.

Experienced professional management. Mutual funds are managed by investment professionals trained to manage securities portfolios. Portfolio managers watch the relevant markets daily, selling securities from or buying securities for their portfolios to attempt to meet each portfolio's stated objective(s).

Mutual fund investment managers receive extensive research information from a variety of sources. The investment manager may employ a full-time research staff, use research information from numerous brokerage firms, or employ independent research firms. Some portfolio managers and research analysts personally visit with corporate managers, economists, and government officials. Many mutual fund companies have research branches in foreign countries or employ international money managers and research firms. Therefore, the portfolio managers have the ability to review in-depth reports about specific stocks and bonds prior to investing in them. The amount of research and market information that a portfolio manager has access to is significantly more than typical individual investors are able to acquire.

Diversification. Mutual funds offer the buyer immediate diversification with even a small amount of money. Investing in mutual funds provides you with a means of investing in a diversified portfolio based on the classification of the mutual fund, its investment objective, and portfolio composition.

You may diversify your own portfolio by investing in both domestic and international funds with a small minimum initial investment. Furthermore, a mutual fund probably exists for almost any type of investment strategy or type of underlying security.

Ease of buying and selling. Each day the New York Stock Exchange is open for business, you are able to purchase or redeem mutual fund shares. The mutual fund's current NAV is the price that you either pay, if purchasing shares, or receive, if redeeming shares. You may not place any limit orders, stop orders, or good-till-cancel orders when purchasing or redeeming mutual fund shares.

Based on the large quantity of securities traded, the mutual fund management company pays commission costs substantially lower than an individual trader would pay. This savings, passed on to investors, is part of your benefit in investing in mutual funds.

Shareholder Services

Mutual funds offer various shareholder services. Review the following services and, when appropriate, take advantage of them.

Reinvestment of income dividends and capital gains. The mutual fund company normally allows you to reinvest income dividends and capital gains distributions in shares of the same fund and, in some cases, in shares of another fund in the same family. Reinvesting dividends and capital gains distributions can add to the total return on your investment. The four alternatives for your dividends and capital gains distributions are:

1. Receive both dividends and capital gains in cash.
2. Receive dividends in cash and reinvest capital gains in shares of the same fund or in shares of another fund in the same family.
3. Receive capital gains in cash and reinvest dividends in shares of the same fund or in shares of another fund in the same family.
4. Reinvest both dividends and capital gains in shares of the same fund or in shares of another fund in the same family.

Direct deposit. Mutual fund companies offer the convenience of directly depositing your distributions in your local bank or brokerage account.

Automatic investment plan. An automatic investment plan is normally available to shareholders, allowing you to invest a fixed amount monthly or quarterly by debiting your checking or savings account. Certain restrictions apply based on minimum investment and initial purchase.

Systematic withdrawal. You may want to establish a *systematic withdrawal plan* that allows you to withdraw a fixed dollar amount on a monthly or quarterly basis. An advantage of using a systematic withdrawal plan is the benefit of receiving regular payments. However, three disadvantages are:

1. The constant buying and redeeming of shares creates additional tax preparation when determining gain or loss for each trade.
2. Redeemed shares may be subject to sales charges.
3. If you withdraw more money than the fund earns through dividends and capital appreciation, part of your payment reduces your principal. If you continually withdraw from your principal, at some point your investment will be gone.

Recordkeeping. Mutual fund management companies supply you with statements showing account information such as the name of the fund, account number, total number of shares owned, NAV, market value of shares, transactions, dividends and distributions paid for the period and year-to-date, dividend and capital gains payment option, and shares held by the fund and/or by you. Some statements show the cost basis of the shares you originally purchased. The cost basis is important when calculating your tax liability for redeemed shares (see Chapter 19).

The statement also displays your name, address, and Social Security or tax identification number. If you find any errors, immediately inform your investment professional, mutual fund management company, or transfer agent. If your Social Security or tax identification number is wrong or not on file, the mutual fund may withhold a portion of the distribution or sale proceeds. The amount withheld is sent to the Internal Revenue Service (IRS) to apply toward your tax liability. If such payment is not due at the time it is withheld, you are not earning interest on the money from that date to the time it is actually due to be paid to the IRS.

Confirmation of trade. After each trade (buy or sell), you receive a confirmation or statement showing the name of the fund, trade date, the number of shares, executed price, total amount of the transaction, and other trade-related information. If you trade the shares through a brokerage firm, a bank with brokerage operations, or a financial planning firm, you will receive a confirmation or statement from the mutual fund company and you also may receive a confirmation from the financial firm.

When you receive the confirmation or statement, check it for accuracy. If a mistake is made or you do not understand the confirmation or statement, call the person with whom you placed the order to review the information. Be sure you retain the confirmation or statement for your tax records.

24-hour account access. Most mutual fund companies provide you with a toll-free number so you may access your account to determine your share balance, the fund's net asset value, distribution schedules and rates, and other pertinent information.

Availability of information. Mutual fund management companies are required to provide shareholders with both an annual and semiannual report. Also, the investment manager usually encloses a letter in the report discussing current market conditions and the performance of the fund. Additional information about the fund's portfolio composition, historical performance of the fund, and comparative market performance may also be reviewed.

Using This Information

Now that you have an overview of the advantages of investing in mutual funds, decisions you must make, and what you can and cannot expect, the following chapters will give you more information about each of these issues. When you finish, you will be able to make more appropriate decisions to meet your investment objectives.

CHAPTER 2

Your Role as an Investor

Investing is unique for each individual. Each person needs to consider personal investment goals and objectives, risk tolerance, return expectations, financial assets, income, age, health, family obligations, and investment experience. These factors together are your *investor's profile*. Because each investor's circumstances are unique and the investment alternatives are numerous, no single investment recommendation is appropriate for everyone.

You must understand the role of the investment professional to determine if you need to employ one. In addition, understanding the organizations involved with mutual funds helps you know with whom and how your money is being invested, managed, and reviewed.

You, the Investor

An informed investor is usually a more successful investor. You do not need to know about every investment in the financial arena. However, you should know and understand the investments you own and those you are contemplating owning. Read the *Wall Street Journal* and the financial pages of your newspaper daily. Also read business and financial periodicals, investment books and brochures, and prospectuses. How much information you need to gather on your own depends on whether you use an investment professional (discussed later in this chapter).

Using your investor's profile, you will consider the investment objective of the particular investment and the risks and returns associated with that investment. Risks and returns (income or growth) will be discussed fully in Chapter 3. Briefly, risk is a measurement of how likely a fund is to reach its stated objectives, based on factors that may impact the underlying funds positively or negatively. Assess risk in relation both to how your principal and investment income are likely to be affected.

Each mutual fund has a set of risk considerations that you should thoroughly understand. How likely is it that the outcome will be positive? If it is, how high will your return be? How likely is it that the outcome will be negative? If it is, will you lose income only, or will you lose principal? Is this investment a good risk to meet your goals? Are your other investments doing well enough that you can afford to lose this one without endangering your overall investment plan? These are the risk questions that need to be addressed—on your own or with your investment professional.

Investment Professional

An investment professional may be a registered representative, registered investment adviser, a certified financial planner. When researching which professional to use (if any), check training, credentials, services offered, hours of service, and charges.

Registered representative. A *registered representative* is an individual who is registered with one of the self-regulatory organizations, such as the New York Stock Exchange (NYSE), American Stock Exchange (AMEX), or the National Association of Securities Dealers (NASD). Registered representatives also are known as stockbrokers, account executives, financial consultants, or investment consultants, depending on the titles given by their respective firms and their investment training and licenses. Registered representatives provide portfolio recommendations and advice for investment and retirement planning to their clients as well as execute buy and sell orders.

Registered investment adviser. A *registered investment adviser* is an individual or firm who is registered with the Securities and Exchange Commission (SEC). A registered investment adviser manages assets, usually on a fee basis. Basically, managing assets means buying and selling securities in a portfolio, when deemed to be appropriate. Mutual funds' investment managers are registered investment advisers.

Certified financial planner. A *certified financial planner* is an individual who is certified by the College of Financial Planning and who advises individuals on investing, in addition to other financial matters such as retirement and estate planning.

Services Offered

Investment professionals may specialize in a certain aspect of the industry or may cover a broad range of services, depending upon their registrations and/or licenses, and their firms' resources. Interview several investment professionals. Look for a person whom you can communicate with, trust, and depend on, and whose professional advice supports your objectives. Be confident that your adviser will give you the proper information and has the expertise to advise you. Your investment professional must be both trustworthy and knowledgable.

The investment professional's role is to know your investor's profile. After discussing that with you, he or she is better able to make an appropriate portfolio recommendation. Together you can establish your investment policy statement. The investment professional should explain to you the investment characteristics, risks, and potential returns for each investment. He or she should also explain to you the costs, fees, investment objectives, and the underlying securities and portfolio composition of the mutual fund being recommended to you. The investment professional can explain the benefits of asset allocation and diversification for your portfolio and why the selected mutual funds are being recommended to you.

Firms That Sell Mutual Funds

You may invest in mutual funds through several types of companies, such as full-service brokerage firms, discount brokerage firms, banks with brokerage operations, financial planning firms, and mutual fund management companies. Mutual fund management companies typically use a distributor to sell their shares.

Full-service brokerage firms. Full-service brokerage firms provide you with a diverse number of investment services. Many of the full service firms have their own proprietary group of mutual funds called a family of funds. In addition, they have selling agreements with numerous other mutual fund management companies or their subsidiaries. Thus, their registered representatives are able to offer you a full line of mutual funds instead of just their own.

Besides giving personal consultations, investment professionals at full-service firms also have access to numerous portfolio management computer programs. The programs are used to help you in investment planning, managing your securities, and allocating your assets. Brokerage firms offer some services based on an annual fee rather than sales charges.

Discount brokerage firms. Some discount brokerage firms offer their own proprietary family of mutual funds, in addition to numerous nonproprietary mutual funds. Services such as portfolio management and mutual fund selection computer programs may be available. The programs help you to select investments, manage your securities, and allocate your assets.

Banks with brokerage operations. Banks that have brokerage operations may offer full or discount service. Some banks have their own proprietary family of mutual funds. In addition, they have selling agreements with numerous other mutual fund management companies or their subsidiaries. Banks also may offer portfolio management and mutual fund selection computer programs.

Financial planning firms. Some firms, such as financial planning firms, charge a fee based on the assets under management or assets reviewed. The fee may be a percentage of the assets or a flat fee for different sizes of accounts.

Typically, financial planning firms do not have their own proprietary family of mutual funds. They may offer a variety of funds from mutual fund management companies as well as portfolio management and mutual fund selection computer programs.

Mutual fund management companies. You can purchase and redeem shares directly with some mutual fund management companies or their subsidiaries without going through another financial institution. Typically, you must decide what fund to buy, when to buy it, and when to redeem it. Developing your own portfolio and continually monitoring it are your responsibilities.

Some mutual fund management companies have personnel who are registered with one of the self-regulatory organizations. Also, they may provide you with the tools for you to do your own portfolio analysis and mutual fund selection.

Distributors. A distributor, usually organized as a subsidiary of the investment management company, is an organization that sells shares to the public or to other broker-dealers (brokerage firms) on a continual basis. A distributor may enter into selling agreements with selected brokerage firms who in turn sell shares to the public. The distributor, also known as the fund *underwriter,* is paid a fee for selling shares of the fund and for sales-related expenses. The plan of distribution in the prospectus states the sales charges and 12b-1 distribution fees, if any, and how they are calculated.

Online computer services. More and more brokerage firms and mutual fund management companies offer access to their services and funds via online computer service. Usually, you must do your own research, asset allocation, and mutual fund selection. Information on the Internet is prolific and very useful. However, information on the Internet is not regulated. Therefore, as Mary L. Shapiro, president of NASD Regulation, Inc. (NASDR) said, "We want to raise awareness of the need for the buyer to beware when it comes to trading stocks based on message postings. Investors need to realize that while they might be reading honest conversations, they could just as easily be looking at the work of a corporate insider, stock promoter, or short seller using an alias to deceive the unsuspecting or to manipulate the market."

Investment Manager

The investment manager provides the organizational structure for the family of mutual funds. The responsibilities of the investment manager are stated in the investment advisory agreement. The role of the investment manager is to serve the mutual fund as an adviser, manager, or administrator. Each fund has operating officers to manage the daily business activities.

The investment manager assures shareholders that the portfolio manager is investing the fund's assets according to the investment objective in the prospectus. Also, the investment manager tries to provide competitive investment returns, easy-to-read statements, and information about the mutual funds.

Directors or Trustees

The mutual fund's board of directors or trustees review the performance of the fund and services to the shareholders, review distributions to the shareholders, and ensure the mutual fund is being operated under applicable federal and state regulations.

Portfolio Manager

The portfolio manager decides which securities to buy or sell, at what price, and how many. The portfolio manager may buy only securities that meet the investment objectives set forth in the mutual fund's prospectus. Many funds are judged by the reputation, quality, and success of the portfolio manager. Sometimes a portfolio manager is hired by a subadviser (see below).

Subadviser

Some investment managers hire another firm, known as a *subadviser,* to manage the fund's portfolio and provide investment advice. Subadvisers are used many times when the investment manager is offering an international or special type of mutual fund. The portfolio manager, who manages the underlying securities on a daily basis, often is employed by the subadviser.

Other organizations, such as the custodian, transfer agent, dividend disbursing agent, and independent accountants provide the mutual fund with specialized services (see Chapter 6).

Professional Advice: Do You Need It?

With the abundance of information available today, many investors wonder if paying an investment professional is cost-effective. Should you do your own research, analysis, asset allocation, portfolio management, and performance review or have an investment professional assist you? To help decide, let's discuss the advantages and disadvantages of using an investment professional.

Your Investment Strategy

To pursue financial security, a well-defined investment policy statement describing your investment objectives, acceptable risks, and expected returns should be written. Over your lifetime, your goals and investment objectives, as well as your investor's profile, change. The economy, interest rates, political environment, stock and bond markets, and tax laws also are constantly changing. Because of these varying factors, it is even more important and challenging to have an overall concise, comprehensive investment strategy. One must consider all the risks and characteristics of each investment alternative, understand the numerous individual investments and their respective markets, and create and maintain an appropriate investment strategy—one of the most difficult challenges one faces during one's lifetime.

The Investment Universe

Today, you can choose from more than 10,000 mutual funds (including the different share classes), in addition to tens of thousands of individual stocks and bonds. Researching, analyzing, and understanding all these mutual funds is a formidable task. Almost every fund has a unique investment objective along with a distinct portfolio composition. The mutual fund's underlying securities have specific risks associated with them. Each portfolio manager has an individualistic style or discipline when it comes to managing a portfolio of stocks, bonds, and money market securities. Families of funds also have different investment philosophies for their own mutual funds. Each mutual fund is sold under its own cost structure, which may include sales charges, fees, and expenses.

Many well-balanced portfolios contain investments in foreign markets. International companies are influenced by economic, social, and political issues. Investing internationally also means understanding the foreign currency exchange's impact on foreign investments. See Financial Focus 3 in Appendix B for a brief discussion about international economics.

To Use or Not to Use an Investment Professional

If you have the means, time, knowledge, and interest to obtain the necessary facts about the various mutual funds and other securities, then you should use many of the public resources and invest without the use of professional investment advice. However, if you need assistance in your own asset allocation and mutual fund selection, you should consider using an investment professional.

DALBAR, Inc. is a full-service information resource firm for the mutual fund industry. Since 1986, DALBAR has published a series of periodicals, industry surveys, and research studies regarding mutual funds' services and customers' satisfaction. According to *DALBAR 1996 Series on Personal Financial Advice, Demand for Personal Financial Advisers,* 89 percent of consumers surveyed felt the need for a personal financial adviser for assets of $100,000 or more. This finding contradicts the popular notion that more and more investors are choosing to "do it themselves." (Source: DALBAR, Inc., Boston, Mass.)

According to the *DALBAR Special Report, Quantitative Analysis of Investor Behavior Study* performed for the period of January 1, 1984–December 31, 1995, investors who used investment professionals outperformed nonusers by more than 16 percent in equity funds and 30 percent in fixed-income funds. The study showed that the advantage is traceable directly to longer retention periods and reduced reaction to changes in market conditions. The fees and expenses paid to an investment professional for advice may well be worth the costs when balanced against the greater returns. Of course, past performance is not a guarantee of future results.

According to the report, actively trading (buying and selling) in mutual funds reduces investment returns. A simple "buy and hold" strategy outperformed the average investor by 3 to 1 over the 12-year period. If market volatility leads you to make snap decisions, you may need an investment professional to help evaluate market conditions.

Using the Investment Professional

The investment professional (choose one who is trained extensively) should be able to assist you in establishing your investor's profile, organizing an investment plan, allocating assets, selecting appropriate mutual funds, and monitoring your portfolio, among other services.

Time-saving service. Your investment professional is only a telephone call away and in most cases you may visit him or her on the same or next day.

Regular portfolio monitoring. Even though mutual funds are typically held long-term, your holdings need to be monitored on a regular basis. One of your investment professional's services is to monitor those investments and inform you when an adjustment to your portfolio may be beneficial.

Risk analysis. Your understanding of risk, as reviewed in Chapter 3, is paramount for you to be an informed mutual fund investor. Mutual funds are neither guaranteed nor insured, and are subject to investment risk. Ask your investment professional to discuss the risks associated with each mutual fund in which you are interested or invested. Do you understand the risk and the potential losses that may arise should the investment not perform as expected?

Return expectation. Knowing your potential return is as important as knowing the risk associated with that return. Expected capital appreciation of any mutual fund, however, is always an educated guess—not a guarantee. Income projections are usually based on the most recent income returns. Your investment professional should discuss the potential returns based on the market outlook, but past performance does not forecast future performance.

Knowledge of fund's portfolio manager. Your investment return is based on the performance of the securities held by the mutual fund. Therefore, your investment professional should discuss the portfolio manager's credentials and investment discipline so you can decide if you are comfortable with the person who is/will be managing your money.

Creating an investor's profile. Before the investment professional recommends a mutual fund to you, and before you buy a mutual fund, you and your investment professional should understand your own investor's profile. (As stated at the beginning of this chapter, your investor's profile includes your investment goals and objectives, risk tolerance, expected returns, time horizon for investing, financial assets, investment experience, income, age, health, and family obligations.) Together you will be able to put together a well-designed investment plan with appropriate mutual funds.

Portfolio management. Asset allocation and diversification are two important portfolio management techniques. Your investment professional will assist you in implementing proper portfolio management strategies to help you achieve your financial goals.

Account servicing. Accuracy is paramount when it comes to recording financial transactions. Your investment professional should review each order for accuracy as to price, quantity, fund, and dividend payment option. Also, if any errors inadvertently occur on your statement, he or she should inform his or her firm of the error so it may be corrected. Even with the advanced technology that financial firms use, occasionally adjustments need to be made to rectify an erroneous entry. Your professional must make certain that all your research and investment discussions are not undone by a clerical error.

Shareholder services. Your investment professional will review your shareholder services such as automatic purchase plan, exchange privilege, reinvestment of dividends and distributions, rights of accumulation, and systematic withdrawal plan.

Specific recommendations. Most investors want specific recommendations from their investment professional, especially because there are more than 10,000 mutual funds to select. Obviously, no one person can know everything about every fund. However, your investment professional should know several funds very well. He or she should know the fund's past performance, types of underlying securities, investment objective, investment manager, and risks associated with the underlying securities. With this in-depth knowledge, the investment professional should make specific recommendations to you that are suitable for your portfolio. The recommendation should provide one or two specific funds and families of funds.

Provides explanations of recommendations and other alternatives. According to *DALBAR 1996 Series on Personal Financial Advice, Customer Expectations of Personal Financial Advisers* study, investors and prospective investors expect their personal financial advisers to educate them about investments and to minimize their taxes. These functions are expected by more than 80 percent of the group surveyed.

Portfolio adjustments. Throughout your years of investing, adjustments to your investment portfolio may need to be made because of changes in the economy and market conditions, investment goals, health, age, employment, and financial condition. Your investment professional should be prepared to discuss the changes and make recommendations to adjust your portfolio to meet your changing situation.

Opportunity phone call. Your investment professional may call you when he or she sees an opportunity to make a potentially profitable investment. The markets are always changing and it may be worthwhile to receive a telephone call from your investment professional when an appropriate opportunity arises.

Retirement planning. Your investment professional should be capable of discussing retirement planning issues with you in the context of your overall investment plans.

Research information. Many investment professionals work for major brokerage firms or brokerage divisions of banks. These firms usually maintain a large research staff or have access to research information. The information includes, but is not limited to, research reports on mutual funds, individual stocks and bonds, other marketable investments, economic conditions, and the stock and bond markets. Information about specific industries and the stock and bond markets in general can be very useful when purchasing mutual funds whose investment strategies include those securities.

Investment planning. Other topics such as estate planning, taxes, and business planning may be discussed with your investment professional along with your attorney and accountant to make a comprehensive financial plan for all of your assets.

Decision making. When making investment decisions, emotional factors such as fear and greed sometimes adversely affect the decisions. Your investment professional may help you make more rational decisions based on fundamentals rather than on emotions.

Personalized service. You may meet with your investment professional personally. He or she performs services for your account based on your individual needs. Unlike other professions, your investment professional normally does not charge you by the hour. You usually may meet with him or her as many times as you like. Most investment professionals receive compensation in the form of sales credits and fees based on the mutual fund transaction and/or the mutual fund assets under management.

Supervisory regulations. Your investment professional is supervised by the appropriate regulatory organization's and his or her firm's operating procedures.

Not Using the Investment Professional

If you have the time, energy, knowledge, and means to manage your own portfolio, many sources of information are available to you. Some of them are:

- Mutual fund research companies
- Television's 24-hour business channels and regularly-scheduled investment news programs

- Talk radio investment programs
- Advertisements about mutual funds and other investments
- Business magazines discussing mutual funds, portfolio management, economic conditions, stock and bond markets
- Daily and weekly newspapers covering the market and economic news
- Investment newsletters
- "Pages" about mutual funds and other investment information on the Internet, also known as the World Wide Web or just Web
- Books

All of these sources provide an abundance of analysis, information, recommendations, and reviews that you can use to enhance your investment knowledge and manage your portfolio. For years, and more so now than ever before, the public resources are available for you to use if you are so inclined. Whether you rely on an investment professional or do your own portfolio management, these public resources can be very beneficial in helping you become a more educated investor. Investment professionals use the same resources to update and increase their knowledge of the investment business.

Remember, however, that these sources are giving general information, not specific advice for your particular investment objectives or portfolio. No single magazine, television show, or Internet page can address risk and return expectation for your investor's profile.

CHAPTER 3

Understanding Risks and Returns

Most people realize that investing is a risky business, but they often don't identify precisely the diversity of perils that a particular investment faces. Every investment has risks associated with it. Understanding risks helps you make better investment decisions and may give you the comfort level to hold a certain investment during an adverse time to improve your long-term return and minimize charges and fees.

Types of Risks

When you invest, be alert to the 12 major risks described below (other risks also may exist). However, with proper diversification, you can guard against overexposure to any one risk and maximize the possibility of long-term returns to your overall portfolio.

1. Inflation risk. *Inflation risk* is also known as *purchasing power risk*. Rising prices will reduce the purchasing power of a dollar. For example, if the Consumer Price Index (CPI) has a 5 percent annual inflation rate for 15 years, it will cut the buying power of $1,000 to $481. Overly cautious investors who keep all their assets in lower-yielding investments such as savings accounts and money market funds may not earn enough to outpace rising prices. In addition, rising inflation reduces the value of future income from investments with fixed-income payments, such as long-term bonds.

2. Interest rate risk. The *interest rate* is the *price of money.* When interest rates change, investors may sell one investment and buy another, causing prices to move. Rising interest rates cause fixed-income investments to decrease in price. Higher interest rates make yields on existing bonds less attractive, so their market values decline. And rising rates also may make stocks less attractive by making their dividend yields look less valuable and, over the long run, decrease profitability of the underlying companies. Investors who borrow money from brokerage firms to purchase stocks face higher borrowing costs as interest rates rise.

3. Economic risk. *Economic risk* comes from two sources. First, slower economic growth may cause investment instruments to fall in price. Shares of growth companies may decline because they require an expanding economy to sustain their earning gains. Second, cyclical companies such as automakers and chemical producers usually cannot cut costs or streamline operations to counteract a decline in revenues during a recession, so their shares may decline as well. Economic downturns also can undercut financially weak firms and their low-quality bonds might default.

4. Market risk. *Market risk* reflects the price fluctuation of an investment. The price increases or decreases based on the supply and demand for the security. Factors causing the change in value may be real or they may be related to the expectations of buyers and sellers. Such factors as economic and governmental policies, unrest overseas, tax law changes, trade agreements, and computerized program trading all may contribute to market volatility. Investor psychology or attitude also may affect the performance of investment markets, either positively or negatively.

5. Specific risk. *Specific risk* covers events that may affect only a particular company or industry. For example, the death of a company's founder could send the stock price down. Specific risk also includes the possibility that government regulations will harm a particular group of companies, that technological advances will push a company to the forefront or set an industry into long-term decline, or that new competitors will force profit margins down.

6. Marketability risk. *Marketability risk* results from a person's inability to sell the investment. If the investment has appreciated in value but cannot be sold, the value cannot be realized; thus, the investor faces the risk that the value may fall in the future. Lack of liquidity may cause the investor to accept a lower price than the true value of the investment, rather than have the price fall even further.

7. Taxation risk. *Taxation risk* results from the possibility that the government changing the tax laws will affect a particular investment. A new tax law may cause the investment's net profitability to be less than it was under the old law.

8. Financial risk or credit risk. *Financial risk* or *credit risk* results from the issuer's possible inability to turn a profit and remain in business to meet its financial obligations. For example, with bonds, the financial risk or credit risk is whether the issuer can make interest and principal payments to the bondholder. Stocks have financial risk associated with the issuing companies staying profitable and paying dividends to the shareholders, or even existing in business.

9. Currency risk. *Currency risk* exists when you invest in foreign securities or securities denominated in foreign currency. The value of a mutual fund's underlying foreign investments are affected by changes in currency exchange rates. The United States dollar value of a foreign security decreases when the value of the United States dollar rises against the foreign currency in which the security is denominated. The United States dollar value of a foreign security increases when the value of the United States dollar falls against the foreign currency in which the security is denominated. Currency risk is also known as *foreign exchange* risk. Another component of currency risk is the impact of currency controls by foreign governments. Refer to Chapter 16 and Financial Focus 3 in Appendix B for more discussion on currency risk.

10. Political risk. *Political risk* exists when a foreign country is socially, economically, or politically unstable or the governing laws are changed which adversely affect a specific investment. Additionally, the foreign government may impose excessive taxes and limit or prevent the transfer of the fund's assets out of the country. Political risk is difficult to estimate because no one knows when laws will be changed or when a politically volatile situation will affect the marketplace.

11. International risk. *International risk* exists due to difficulties of knowing and interpreting financial and economic information. International companies are not subject to the same accounting standards and practices as are United States companies. Additionally, trading foreign securities may have both higher commission rates, custodian fees, taxes, and less regulation than trading United States securities. International securities may be less liquid and more volatile than domestic securities. Besides currency risk (see 9), the cost of currency conversion may impact the return of international securities' return.

12. Reinvestment risk. *Reinvestment risk* occurs when an investment returns either principal or income that needs to be reinvested at the prevailing interest rate. If interest rates are lower at the time of reinvestment, the investor will be adversely affected.

Always consider the risk and return of an investment. *The greater the risk, the greater the **potential** return and the greater the **potential** loss.*

Types of Returns

People invest in the securities markets for a variety of reasons. As discussed earlier, their investment objectives are usually preservation of capital, generating income, and/or capital appreciation. In Chapter 10, you will review the rate of return you want to achieve. A progress report usually helps determine whether you are on track in attaining your goal. Calculating your distribution rate, capital appreciation or loss, and total return are necessary check points on the way to evaluating your progress toward your overall investment objective. Annualizing your returns will allow you to compare your returns to those of alternative investments.

Distributions

Mutual funds make *distributions* to you in the form of income dividends and capital gains, either short-term or long-term. A mutual fund receives income, such as dividends and interest, from the securities held in its portfolio. After the fund has paid its expenses, it distributes the net income, if any, to you. The income return, expressed as a percentage yield, is important for you to know so you may compare the fund's return to that of alternative investments. (The Securities and Exchange Commission (SEC) standardized the reporting of "yields" on mutual fund shares.) Capital gains are distributed to you when the fund realizes a net profit from trading securities within the fund's portfolio.

Cash dividends. Mutual funds can declare dividends daily, monthly, quarterly, semiannually, or annually, depending on the fund type. You may receive the dividends in cash or have the fund automatically reinvest the cash dividend in more shares or sometimes in shares of another fund in the same family of funds, usually without a sales charge. Whether you receive the cash dividends or reinvest them in more shares, you must declare the dividends as income—either taxable or tax-exempt—on your tax return.

Capital gains. When the fund sells securities and realizes a net profit, you will receive that profit in a capital gains distribution. If the gain is considered long term, you must declare it as a long-term capital gain on your tax return. If the gain is considered short term, you must declare it as income on your tax return. Of course, you may receive the cash, or have the fund reinvest either type of distribution into more shares or sometimes in shares of another fund in the same family of funds, usually without a sales charge. Check with your tax adviser for further information regarding the tax consequences of mutual funds distributions.

You realize a profit or loss when you sell your shares, depending upon the difference between your adjusted cost basis and the net proceeds, excluding any dividends and capital gains paid to you.

Standardized Numbers

In 1988, the SEC adopted a standardized yield formula (the *SEC Yield)* and total return (the *SEC Standardized Total Return*) to establish a uniform basis for reporting the income and total return performance, respectively, of mutual funds.

SEC Yield. The purpose of the SEC Yield is to increase the investor's ability to compare and evaluate the income performance regardless of how a fund distributes its net investment income. The SEC Yield is similar to a yield to maturity, whereas the fund's distribution rate is similar to a current yield. The SEC Yield formula uses an approximate, theoretical current income derived from the portfolio of securities after expenses. The income is calculated over a 30-day base period and divided by the current offering price. This figure is compounded monthly for a six-month period and then annualized. The resulting percentage is the SEC Yield. The formula does not include any realized gains from portfolio transactions.

Standardized SEC Total Return. Because the SEC Yield and the distribution rate often differ, a better calculation may be the total return of the fund. The calculation for total return uses both income received (or reinvested) plus capital appreciation or loss over a period of specified years less sales charges.

Total return is the figure you most need to review and analyze the fund's performance. This figure tells you whether your investment is making money or losing money after all income earned and capital appreciation or depreciation. Total return should be viewed over a number of years—one year, five years, and ten years—or over the life of the fund. A good return one year doesn't mean similar returns over longer periods either in the past or future.

Management fees, operating expenses, and 12b-1 distribution fees are deducted from the fund's assets prior to calculating the standardized numbers.

Nonstandardized Numbers

Distribution rate. The distribution rate formula uses the current net investment income paid to you. This figure is then annualized and divided by the fund's current offering price. The distribution rate may include short-term capital gains, which may or may not be realized in the future. Therefore, using only the net investment income provides a more meaningful estimate of the current distribution rate.

Nonstandardized yield. The nonstandardized yield may use the previous 12 months of dividends divided by the current offering price.

Nonstandardized total return. The calculation for total return uses both income received (or reinvested) plus capital appreciation or loss over a period of specified years, without consideration for any sales charges when buying or selling.

Total return is the figure you need most to review and analyze the fund's performance. This figure tells you whether your investment is making money or losing money after all income earned and capital appreciation or depreciation is figured. Management fees, operating expenses and 12b-1 distribution fees are deducted from the fund's assets prior to calculating the nonstandardized numbers.

CHAPTER 4

Understanding the Prospectus and Annual Reports

Reading the prospectus and annual and semiannual reports carefully makes you more knowledgeable about your investment. The prospectus could be called the owner's manual for your mutual fund. Keep your prospectus on file and when you want to know something about your mutual fund, review the prospectus to obtain the necessary information. Your investment professional is conversant about the basic content of a prospectus if you have questions. Most mutual fund companies provide an investment guide or brochure along with the prospectus, which is helpful to further understand the mutual fund investment.

The annual report includes a variety of financial reports about the fund's performance that have been audited by a certified public accountant (CPA) for accuracy. The financial reports are usually accompanied by explanations for the fund's performance, including a comparison to the market in general.

Prospectus

The prospectus has two parts: the prospectus and the statement of additional information. The fund is required to give the investor a current prospectus prior to or by settlement date of purchase. Investors must request the statement of additional information however.

The prospectus lists, among other information, the mutual fund's investment objective, risk considerations, fees, expenses, investment manager, shareholder services, and type of underlying securities. Below is the basic information found in most prospectuses.

Table of Contents

The table of contents provides you with a quick reference as to where information is found in the prospectus. Familiarize yourself with the format of the prospectus.

Disclaimers

The following seven disclaimers are important to know:

1. Shares of the fund are not deposits, or obligations of, or guaranteed or endorsed by, any bank, and the shares are not federally insured by the Federal Deposit Insurance Corporation, the Federal Reserve Board, or any other government agency.
2. These securities have not been approved or disapproved by the Securities and Exchange Commission (SEC) or any state securities commission, nor has the SEC or any state securities commission passed upon the accuracy or adequacy of this prospectus. Any representation to the contrary is a criminal offense.
3. There is no assurance that the fund's investment objective will be achieved.
4. Investments in the fund are subject to investment risks, including possible loss of principal.
5. Money market funds attempt to maintain a stable net asset value of $1 per share. However, there can be no assurance that it will succeed in doing so.
6. Read the prospectus before investing and keep it for further reference.

7. Past performance is no guarantee of future results.

Prospectus Summary

Some prospectuses provide a summary page that briefly lists the fund's investment objective, underlying securities, investment manager, fees, expenses, and risks. Review this page and then proceed to read in detail the remaining information.

Summary of Fund Expenses

Another summary page discusses the sales charges, redemption fees, management fees, and 12b-1 fees, if any. An example is given to illustrate the expenses associated with a hypothetical $1 thousand purchase assuming a 5 percent annual return and redemption at the end of each time period for one, three, or more years. The purpose of the example is to assist the investor in understanding the various costs and expenses that an investor in the fund will bear. The example should not be considered a representation of past or future expenses, as actual expenses may be greater or less than those shown. Study this page and you will better understand what you are paying for when buying, holding, and selling shares in this mutual fund. Although fees and expenses are important, understanding the investment objective and risks is more important.

Financial Highlights

The financial highlights section shows, usually in table form, financial information for the past ten years or since the inception of the fund, whichever is shortest. The information includes the following ten items:

1. Beginning net asset value for the year
2. Net investment income
3. Net realized and unrealized gain and loss
4. Dividends and distributions
5. Ending net asset value for the year
6. Total investment return
7. Expense ratio

8. Net investment income ratio
9. Total net assets
10. Portfolio turnover rate

A review of these figures provides you with the past annual performance of and financial information about the mutual fund. The total investment return does not include any sales charges. Furthermore, the total investment return can be used when comparing the fund's performance to the appropriate mutual fund index or market index.

The Fund and Its Management

This section explains the fund's organization, investment manager, portfolio manager, subadviser (if any), and compensation of the investment manager.

Investment Objective and Policies

Of all sections, this is the most important one for you to read and understand. The investment objective and types of securities allowed to be purchased are explained in detail. Specific investment policies regarding the percent of total assets that may be purchased in each type of security is discussed. Specific types of transactions to implement the management of the portfolio is reviewed. The methodology of managing the portfolio is discussed, along with the name and credentials of the portfolio manager(s). Risk considerations are explained in detail. Even though the portfolio may not currently contain all of the securities or types of transactions listed, it is worthwhile to know what is available for use by the portfolio manager. A fund's annual or semiannual report will show which securities the mutual fund owned on the reporting date.

Investment Restrictions

According to the Investment Company Act of 1940, certain types of mutual funds are limited in the amount and types of securities that may be held, based on the fund's total assets. This section discusses those restrictions and any other portfolio guidelines.

Purchase of Fund Shares

This section describes the method of purchasing shares of the fund, including the minimum purchase, the company who is selling the shares (the distributor), compensation to the distributor, and the plan of distribution. The *plan of distribution* states if the shares are being sold with a front-end sales charge, contingent deferred sales charge, level-load, or no-load. The plan of distribution also discusses any 12b-1 fees and redemption fees.

Calculation of Net Asset Value

This section discusses how the net asset value (NAV) is determined.

Redemptions

The redemption section discusses the specific sales charges and fees, if any, when you redeem your shares. This section also explains any exemptions from the charges.

Shareholder Services

Shareholder services include the following six services:

1. Reinvestment of income dividends and capital gains in more shares of the fund or of another fund in the same family of funds
2. Automatic purchase plan that provides a transfer of money from a checking or savings account to purchase shares of a fund on a periodic basis, such as monthly or quarterly
3. Systematic withdrawal plan, whereby a shareholder receives a check for a specified amount, either monthly or quarterly, from income, capital gains, or liquidation of shares from the fund
4. 24-hour telephone access
5. Direct deposit of distributions into your checking account
6. Exchange privilege, allowing the shareholder to exchange shares of one fund for shares in another fund in the same family with typically the same pricing structure, without a sales charge

Dividends, Distributions, and Federal Income Taxation

Knowing how the fund pays dividends and distributions helps you understand your investment. You should consult your tax adviser regarding the taxability of dividends and distributions to see if an individual fund fits in your overall investment strategy.

Performance Information

The fund may quote its total return in advertisements and sales literature. This section tells you how the fund calculates that return.

Other Information

This section covers the confirmations and statements for shareholders' transactions. Also, this section provides the name of the transfer agent, custodian, legal counsel, and independent accountants, along with procedures for shareholder inquiries.

Supplement to Current Prospectus

Occasionally, the fund's current prospectus is revised prior to the required annual update. If so, a supplement is sent to the shareholders describing the changes. Changes to a prospectus could include a new portfolio manager or change in dividend payment schedule. Material changes, such as changing the investment objective, require a vote by shareholders.

Statement of Additional Information

The statement of additional information is a separate document that describes in more detail the information listed in the prospectus. If you want more specific information about the mutual fund and the investment manager, request and read the statement of additional information.

Investment Guide

Most mutual fund companies provide an investment guide, sometimes known as a product guide, that accompanies the prospectus. The investment guide usually presents the mutual fund from a portfolio management approach. It also reviews some of the same information the prospectus contains. The investment guide is typically easier to read and understand than the prospectus. Read both the investment guide and the prospectus to get a more complete understanding of the mutual fund. An investment guide must be accompanied by a prospectus. Some mutual fund management companies publish the prospectus and investment guide as one brochure.

Profile Prospectus

According to the Investment Company Institute, in August 1995 the SEC approved use by several participating fund groups for a one-year trial of prototype versions of the prospectus known as a profile prospectus. The Investment Company Institute is the national trade association for the investment company industry. A *profile prospectus,* sometimes called a *short prospectus,* is a condensed version of the standard mutual fund prospectus. The profile prospectus addresses 11 critical areas:

1. The fund's goals or objectives
2. The fund's investment strategies
3. The fund's risks
4. The kind of investor for whom the fund might be an appropriate investment
5. A table showing fees and expenses of the fund
6. A bar chart showing the fund's total return in each of the past ten years, accompanied by standardized SEC performance data of the fund
7. The name of the fund's investment adviser
8. How investors may purchase shares of the fund
9. How investors may redeem their shares
10. When and how distributions are made by the fund
11. Other services the fund offers to investors

At the time of this book's printing, the SEC is considering a rule change to permit the use of the profile prospectus throughout the industry.

Plain-English Prospectus

Another change in the standard prospectus is the advent of the plain-English prospectus. The *plain-English* prospectus is designed to allow the investor to read and understand the information presented by writing it in everyday language without the investment-industry jargon. At the time of this book's printing, the SEC is considering a rule change to permit the use of the plain-English prospectus throughout the industry.

Key Information about the Fund

Retain the fund's prospectus for future reference. Once you have purchased a mutual fund, in addition to knowing the firm you purchased the mutual fund through, you should know some key items to help you follow your mutual fund investment.

Mutual fund group. Knowing the fund group (family of funds) allows you to find the group in the newspaper or discuss it with your investment professional.

Complete mutual fund name and share class. Knowing the complete name and share class, if applicable, will help you distinguish your fund from all the others.

Symbol. Most firms usually execute buy and sell orders of mutual funds using symbols. The typical mutual fund symbol consists of five letters, generally ending with an *X*.

CUSIP number. The CUSIP (Committee for Uniform Security Identification Procedures) number identifies each marketable security. By knowing the CUSIP number, you will always be able to find the mutual fund's correct name.

✏️ Your Investor's Guide

Key Information about Your Mutual Fund

Mutual Fund Group _____

Mutual Fund Name _____

Share Class, if applicable _____

Symbol _____

CUSIP Number _____

Newspaper Abbreviation _____

Newspaper abbreviation. The newspaper abbreviation is important because many fund families have numerous funds that have somewhat similar names. The fund's newspaper abbreviation is not the same as the fund's symbol.

Complete the above Your Investor's Guide to help you keep track of your specific mutual fund(s).

Annual and Semiannual Reports

Mutual fund companies are minimally required to send you a semiannual report and an audited annual report. An annual report may include a letter to the shareholder from the Chairman of the Board or President, a list of securities held in the portfolio, financial statements, and notes to the financial statements. Some annual reports are bare-bone efforts, while others may be slick, photo-filled publications. The form is not as important as the content.

Letter to the Shareholder

The shareholder letter explains the fund's performance for the past accounting period, the general market performance compared to the fund's performance, any special economic or market-related activities that affected the fund's performance, portfolio adjustments and the outlook for the fund, plus the economy and the marketplace. This letter should explain the fund's recent activities and performance. If you have further questions, ask your investment professional for more detailed explanations.

Portfolio Securities

Annual reports and most semiannual reports list the fund's securities held as well as each fund's percentage of the portfolio, and the quantity and market value for each. Throughout the year, the portfolio manager buys and sells securities, so by the time the reports are produced, printed, and distributed, the portfolio holdings in the reports may not be current. Because the portfolio manager's purchases are restricted by the fund's objectives and profile, however, the current holdings will be very similar to what is in the annual report.

Financial Statements

The annual and semiannual reports contain financial reports that allow the investor to see the current state of the fund as well as track its performance.

Statement of Assets and Liabilities. The Statement of Assets and Liabilities is the same as the fund's balance sheet that shows both total assets and total liabilities. The difference between total assets and total liabilities is the *net assets* of the fund. The net assets divided by the number of shares outstanding provides you with the *net asset value* as of the date of the report.

Statement of Operations. The Statement of Operations is the same as an income statement. It shows the total income, total expenses, net realized gain or loss, and the net change in unrealized appreciation or depreciation. The sum of these figures indicates the net increase or decrease in the fund's operations for a certain period of time such as the past 12 or 6 months, depending on the type of report.

Statement of Changes in Net Assets. The Statement of Changes in Net Assets shows the change of net assets from one period to the next period such as the past twelve months, six months, or three months, depending on the type of report. The net change is a reflection of net investment gain or loss, net change in unrealized appreciation or depreciation, and distributions from net realized gains.

Financial Highlights. The Financial Highlights report summarizes all of the above. This report shows the change in net asset value, net investment income, net realized and unrealized gain or loss, and distributions for the most recent period and usually for several prior years (usually for ten years if the fund has been operating that long). Additionally, the Financial Highlights report may show the total investment return, expense ratio, portfolio turnover rate, and average commission rate paid. The *income ratio* is calculated by dividing net investment income by annual average net assets and multiplying by 100 to express it as a percent. The income ratio would be relatively low for growth-oriented funds and relatively high for income-oriented funds. The *expense ratio* is calculated by dividing the total annual expense by the average annual net assets and multiplying by 100 to express it as a percent. The *portfolio turnover rate* is the percent that the total portfolio of securities has been purchased, sold, and repurchased. The *average commission rate paid* is the dollar amount that the fund paid to execute the orders when buying and selling the portfolio securities.

The last three figures allow you to better understand the expenses involved in managing the mutual fund. However, these figures are not solely to be used to determine which mutual fund to buy.

Notes to the Financial Statements

The Notes to the Financial Statements provide additional information about the fund's procedure for valuating the portfolio securities, accounting methods, federal income tax status, and/or dividends and distributions to shareholders. Also, the Note may include information about the investment management agreement, plan of distributing the shares, and security transactions.

Key Points

The key items in the annual and semiannual reports are the letter by the Chairman or President and the list of portfolio securities. Concentrate on these two parts and you will be a better informed investor. The other statements give you information about the fund's performance that will help you decide whether to hold or sell that particular fund.

CHAPTER 5

Buying and Selling Mutual Funds

Open-end mutual funds do not trade on the New York Stock Exchange, American Stock Exchange, The Nasdaq Stock Market, or other exchanges. Orders to purchase or redeem mutual funds are sent to the mutual fund management company for execution prior to the close of each business day (4:00 P.M., eastern standard time). You place an order to purchase or redeem shares with the mutual fund company or through your investment professional. The net asset value (NAV) is calculated by the management company after the close of business each day to determine the price of the fund shares. This NAV is the price you pay for or receive from your shares and is published in the financial periodicals the following day.

Before purchasing shares in a mutual fund, you should know not only the NAV, but the fund's sales charges (either when buying or redeeming), management fees, and annual operating expenses. Understanding the full costs involved makes you a knowledgeable investor.

Initial Public Offering and Continuous Offering

When shares of a mutual fund are sold to the public for the first time, an initial public offering (IPO) takes place. The shares are offered to the public at a predetermined price during the underwriting period, based on the pricing structure of the shares. The underwriting period may be a month or longer and the price is the same for all buyers during that time. After the initial public offering, the net asset value fluctuates based on the performance of the fund's underlying securities.

Usually, after the offering is completed, the mutual fund company temporarily closes the fund to new buyers; this time is called the *cooling-off period*. Several weeks later when the fund reopens for new buyers and usually remains open indefinitely, it is known as a *continuous offering*. Once the fund reopens, redemptions may take place from those investors who previously purchased shares.

Sometimes shares may be offered to the public initially on a continuous basis and an underwriting period is not used.

Pricing Mutual Fund Shares

The NAV fluctuates based on the performance of the underlying securities in the fund. Your purchase or redemption (sale) will be based on the next determined NAV. When you redeem your shares, the NAV may be more or less than you originally paid for them.

Net Asset Value

At the close of business each day, the NAV of every mutual fund is calculated using the formula in Figure 5.1. NAVs are listed in most newspapers, usually under either "mutual funds" or "investment companies."

FIGURE 5.1 Formula for Calculating Net Asset Value

$$\frac{(\text{Fund's total assets} - \text{Fund's total expenses and liabilities})}{\text{Fund's outstanding shares}} = \text{Fund's NAV}$$

The NAVs of each type of United States bond and stock funds and international bond and stock funds fluctuate differently in a given market cycle. Knowing and understanding what type of securities your fund holds helps you compare the performance of your fund to the performance of similar securities and understand the risks associated with your fund. Your knowledge of the underlying securities held in the fund's portfolio helps you understand why your fund's NAV is changing.

Expenses of Owning Mutual Funds

Expenses for managing and implementing the business of investing in a fund's underlying securities include management fees, 12b-1 fees, and commissions. These expenses generally are charged against investment income received from held securities, with the rest of the income paid out as dividends. In the prospectus, you will find a full listing of the fund's total expenses and charges. If the fund doesn't have enough income to pay the expenses, the fund's assets will be charged.

Annual Operating Expenses

Annual operating expenses include management fees, 12b-1 distribution fees, and other expenses.

Management fees. Most funds are charged a *management fee* by the manager for the advice and administration of the funds' assets. The management fee is usually based on a percent of the annual average assets of the fund.

12b-1 distribution fees. Another annual expense may be the *12b-1 distribution fee.* This fee covers the fund's selling costs and service fee for maintaining shareholder accounts and for whatever shareholder services may be offered by that fund.

Other expenses. Each fund has other expenses such as valuating the fund's securities, operating the fund, safekeeping the securities, and hiring transfer agents and independent accountants.

Commissions

Mutual fund companies pay a commission to the executing broker when it buys or sells securities for the fund's portfolio. The total amount of commissions paid is not normally listed in the prospectus or annual reports; however, the average commission rate is generally disclosed.

A portfolio manager who actively trades causes the fund's commission expense to rise; a buy-and-hold type of portfolio manager typically trades less and therefore, the commission expense is lower. Most funds alert shareholders to portfolio turnover in their annual reports. If a manager makes more trades than the norm but the fund's returns are also higher than the norm, shareholders and prospective buyers must reach their own decision on whether the manager is doing a good job and they should own the fund.

Costs of Buying and Selling Mutual Funds

Mutual fund management companies determine how they want to charge you when buying and selling their shares. Classes of shares are used to distinguish different cost structures. Although the mutual fund industry does not have a definitive standard for classifying the different cost structures, most fund companies use similar classifications.

Classes of Shares

Mutual fund management companies can charge you many different ways for buying and selling shares, including these five:

1. Front-end sales charge (FESC)
2. Contingent deferred sales charge (CDSC)
3. Level-load (LL)
4. Institutional
5. No-load (NL)

Mutual fund companies sometimes designate the shares as Class A, B, C, etc., or sometimes with numbers such as Class I, II, III, etc. See the prospectus to understand which system a particular fund uses.

FIGURE 5.2   Formula for Calculating Percent Sales Charge of the Offering

$$\frac{(\text{Offering price per share} - \text{Net asset value})}{\text{Offering price per share}} = \text{Percent sales charge}$$

Front-end sales charge shares. *Front-end sales charge (FESC)* means that you pay a sales charge when you buy the shares and nothing when you redeem them. The *offering price,* paid upon purchase, consists of the NAV plus the sales charge. When you sell (redeem) shares, the price you receive is the NAV. To determine the percent sales charge of the offering price use the formula in Figure 5.2.

The average range of a front-end sales charge fund is typically 3.25 percent to 5.75 percent. Shares of bond funds usually have lower front-end sales charges than shares of stock funds. Shares with a front-end sales charge may be described as Class A or Class I shares. In addition to front-end sales charges, management fees, and other expenses, some funds charge annual 12b-1 distribution fees.

Break-points. When you buy shares of a front-end sales charge fund, the offering price you pay includes a sales charge based on the dollar amount of shares you purchase. The fund designates levels for different dollar amounts at which the sales charge is reduced. Each level is known as a *break-point.* Shares purchased in the amount up to the first level are priced at the *maximum offering price (MOP).* Therefore, the more dollar amount you buy at each break-point level, the less sales charge you pay as a percent of the offering price. Therefore, the offering price is less and the value you retain is more as the dollar amount of the transaction increases. Sales charges are described in the prospectus. Figure 5.3 shows an example of a sales charge schedule for a front-end sales charge fund.

To determine the offering price at different break-point levels, use the formula in Figure 5.4.

When you purchase a front-end sales charge fund, make sure you are not buying it just below the next break-point. It may be worthwhile to invest a little more to get to the next break-point and receive the lower price. Your investment professional should explain the break-point levels to you.

FIGURE 5.3   Example of a Front-end Sales Charge Fund Schedule

Total Amount of Transaction	Sales Charge
Less than $50,000	5.75%
$50,000 but less than $100,000	4.50
$100,000 but less than $250,000	3.50
$250,000 but less than $500,000	2.50
$500,000 but less than $1 million	2.00

Letter of intent. By signing a letter of intent, you pledge to the mutual fund company that you will invest a certain amount over a 13-month period. In doing so, the fund charges you the break-point level sales charge for the total amount you have pledged to invest, even though your initial investment would usually be charged a higher rate. However, if after 13 months you have not invested the agreed upon amount, the fund company refigures the appropriate sales charge based on the lower amount invested. The fund bills you for the extra sales charge or sells some of your shares of the fund to pay the refigured sales charge.

Rights of accumulation. Sometimes when you initially purchase a front-end sales charge fund you are not able to purchase enough shares to get to the next break-point level. However, the mutual fund company maintains your cumulative amount of dollars invested in all of their funds. When you buy enough additional shares for your total cumulative purchases to exceed the next break-point, the fund sells you the additional shares at the lower sales charge. This pricing procedure is known as *rights of accumulation.*

FIGURE 5.4   Formula for Calculating Offering Price at Break-Point Levels

$$\frac{\text{Net asset value}}{(1 - \text{Percent sales charge expressed as decimal number})} = \text{Offering price per share}$$

Contingent deferred sales charge shares. *Contingent deferred sales charge (CDSC)* means that you purchase your shares at NAV, pay no sales charge when you purchase the shares, but pay a sales charge when you redeem shares unless you have held the shares for a specified number of years. Generally, you can redeem your shares purchased from reinvested dividend and capital gains distributions without a sales charge. CDSC shares are also known as *back-end load* shares.

When you sell (redeem) shares, the price you receive is the NAV, less any applicable sales charge. The sales charge for a CDSC fund normally is calculated on a declining scale, whereby the charge declines by a certain percentage each year. Some fund companies use the calendar year for computing the time that the shares are held and other companies use an annual anniversary date of purchase for computing the time. After the allotted time, you incur no sales charge when you redeem shares. Normally, the CDSC is charged only on the original cost of the shares and does not include the appreciation. If, however, the share value has declined from the original cost, the CDSC is charged against the lower market value. Shares purchased through dividend reinvestment or shares held for the allotted time, could be sold without being subject to a sales charge and are known as *free shares.* Generally, the CDSC is waived for redemptions if the shareholder dies or becomes disabled. Restrictions regarding the waiving of CDSC are outlined in the prospectus. Shares sold with a contingent deferred sales charge may be described as Class B or Class II shares. Typically, CDSC funds may charge a 12b-1 fee up to 1 percent, along with management fees and other expenses.

The contingent deferred sales charge may change, depending on how long you hold the shares. Figure 5.5 shows an example of a sales charge schedule for a contingent deferred sales charge fund. The number of years you must have held shares to achieve the lowest charge and how low that charge may go vary from fund to fund.

Some fund companies permit you to redeem up to 10 percent of the account value annually through a systematic withdrawal plan without imposing a contingent deferred sales charge.

Also, some fund companies that offer different classes of shares convert shares that you purchased with a contingent deferred sales charge to another class of shares with typically lower expenses after a holding period of approximately six to ten years. Normally, no sales charge is incurred for the conversion, nor are the shares subject to a

FIGURE 5.5   Example of a Contingent Deferred Sales Charge Fund Schedule

Year Since Purchase	CDSC as a Percent of Amount Redeemed
1	5%
2	4
3	3
4	2
5	2
6	1
7 or more	None

sales charge upon redemption. Tax implications may or may not exist, depending on the type of conversion. Check with your tax adviser for the tax consequences of any exchanges.

Level-load shares. *Level-load (LL)* shares generally impose no sales charges when you buy or sell the shares. The price paid at purchase is the NAV. When you sell (redeem) shares, the price you receive is the NAV. However, you pay a 12b-1 fee while you hold the shares. Typically, level-load funds may charge a 12b-1 fee up to 1 percent, or more. However, some level-load fund shares may have a low CDSC for one year. Level-load funds are usually designated Class C or Class III.

Institutional shares. Institutional shares are generally those representing purchases of $1 million or more. Typically, these shares have no sales charge to buy and no sales charge to sell. However, institutional shares, may or may not have ongoing 12b-1 fees. Institutional shares are generally designated as Class D, Class Y, or Class Z.

No-load shares. *No-load (NL)* shares impose no sales charges when you buy or sell the shares. Both purchase and redeeming price is the NAV. If the 12b-1 distribution fee exceeds .25 percent, the fund cannot call itself a no-load fund. Shares of no-load funds may or may not be designated by a class.

Your Investor's Guide

Share Class and Cost Structure

Mutual Fund Name	Share Class	Cost Structure
_____	_____	_____
_____	_____	_____
_____	_____	_____
_____	_____	_____
_____	_____	_____

Other classes of shares. Some mutual fund companies, when converting existing no-load shares to other classes, may give the former no-load shares a different classification. Also, funds that are closed to new investors may designate their shares as Class T shares or another classification.

Class M shares, also known as *mid-level shares,* have lower front-end sales charges than typical Class A shares. Class M shares generally do not have any redemption fees, but may have a 12b-1 fee.

Completing Your Investor's Guide above will help you compare the mutual funds' share classes and cost structures.

Trade and Settlement Dates

Trade date is the day the order is entered to purchase or sell mutual fund shares. The trade date is up to 4:00 P.M. EST of the date the order is received by phone or mail. Later orders have a trade date of the next business day. *Settlement date* is the date when payment for your purchase of mutual fund shares is due, or the date you receive the sale proceeds from the redemption of your shares.

Transaction through a brokerage firm. Your investment professional will ask you about your investor's profile and your dividend and capital gain distribution preference prior to opening an account for you. You also must have signature(s) on file for the necessary documentation so your investment professional can carry out the transactions you request.

On the trade date your investment professional buys or redeems (sells) mutual fund shares for you, you pay or receive respectively the next determined net asset value for the fund's shares, plus or minus any applicable sales charge. Settlement date for purchases and redemptions is usually three business days after trade date. When buying shares, you must deposit or have on deposit the total cost in your brokerage account by settlement date. When redeeming shares for which you hold the certificates, you must deliver the shares in proper negotiable form to your broker. If shares are held by your brokerage firm, networked between your brokerage firm and the mutual fund transfer agent, or held at the transfer agent with your investment professional designated as the registered representative of record, you can redeem shares by instructing your investment professional. *Networked* means that your mutual fund shares are held at the mutual fund's transfer agent, but appear on your brokerage account statement.

Transaction through a transfer agent. If you transact business directly through the mutual fund's transfer agent, you pay or receive the next determined net asset value for the fund's shares after receipt of your instructions, plus or minus any applicable sales charge. When purchasing shares for the first time, you must send the transfer agent a completed and signed application with your check in the amount of your initial purchase with the proper instructions for the following six items:

1. Personal information and address
2. Designation for registration of the shares
3. Amount of purchase
4. Name of the fund
5. Dividend and capital gain distributions payment option
6. Where you want the certificate sent or if you want the certificate held at the transfer agent

When redeeming shares, the transfer agent normally has seven business days after receipt of the certificate and/or written request in good order to mail you a check for your proceeds.

Exchange Privilege

Mutual fund companies usually permit you to exchange all or a portion of your shares of one fund to shares of another fund in the same "fund family," usually without a sales charge. The exchange price is normally the NAV for each fund. Some restrictions may apply to these exchanges regarding the length of time the shares have been held, total value of your holdings to be exchanged, and pricing structure of the fund (same class of shares).

Exchange privilege allows you to move your assets to a different market if one market sector is not performing well. As with a purchase, you must understand the investment objective, risks, and underlying securities of the new fund you are exchanging into. Your investment professional can advise you on and effect your exchange. If you are handling your own account, a *telephone exchange* permits you to make the exchange by phone. In some cases, however, your exchange order must be in writing to the mutual fund company.

The Internal Revenue Service considers an exchange to be a taxable event because you are in effect selling shares of one fund and buying shares in a different fund. Check with your tax adviser for the tax consequences of any exchanges.

Recalculating Net Asset Value

The NAV may be recalculated when dividends are paid or capital gains are distributed.

Dividend and capital gains distributions. When the fund pays a dividend or capital gains distribution, the total assets of the fund are reduced by the total amount of the distribution. Each year the fund distributes substantially all of the net investment income, realized short-term capital gains, and net realized long-term capital gains. However, the fund may retain all or part of any net long-term capital gains in any year for reinvestment. Typically, bond funds pay income dividends monthly and stock funds pay dividends quarterly, although some pay less frequently. Funds declare dividend or capital gains distributions on a frequency stated in the prospectus.

Mutual funds use two methods to determine shareholders of record for the purpose of paying dividends and distributions: (1) ex-date and (2) daily accrual.

Ex-date fund. An ex-date fund (also known as ex-dividend fund) distributes dividend and capital gains monies periodically. As the fund earns income or realizes capital gains, those changes are reflected in the net asset value. When distributions are paid, a *record date* or *cut-off date* is set to determine which shareholders will receive the distribution. A shareholder must own the fund's shares as of this date to receive the distribution. The *payable date* is later than the record date and determines when the fund's distribution is due to eligible shareholders. According to your previously made instructions, you may receive a check, have the amount credited to your investment account, or purchase additional shares with it. If you reinvest the distributions in additional shares, the *reinvestment date* is usually the same as the payable date.

The *ex-dividend date* is the date on which the buyer of the fund's shares is not entitled to the distribution. On the ex-dividend date, the net asset value is reduced by the amount of the distribution per share. You typically do not want to buy shares of a fund just prior to the ex-dividend date because the net asset value declines by the distribution amount on the ex-dividend date and the distribution you receive may be taxable. Additionally, if the fund is a front-end sales charge fund, you are paying a sales charge on an amount that you are about to receive as a distribution.

Daily accrual dividend fund. A daily accrual dividend fund declares dividends daily. Technically, this type of fund does not have an ex-date for distributions. The fund declares a payable date and you receive income dividends based on the number of days you owned shares during that period multiplied by the number of shares. The fund's NAV is not reduced when the fund pays a dividend distribution because the income is not considered part of the fund's assets. Capital gains distributions are declared separately and do have an ex-date. Some bond funds and all money market funds are daily accrual dividend funds.

CHAPTER 6

Management Structures of Mutual Funds

The management structures of mutual funds differ from one fund to another. However, the typical organization structure of a mutual fund management company consists of some or all of the following entities:

- Board of directors or trustees
- Officers
- Investment manager
- Investment adviser
- Subadviser
- Portfolio manager(s)

Other support and service entities include:

- Transfer agent
- Dividend disbursing agent
- Custodian
- Independent accountants

The management style of each fund's portfolio differs based on the fund's investment objective, investment restrictions, and the prescribed investment discipline of the portfolio manager(s). The fund adopts the investment objective and investment restrictions as fundamental policies of the fund and generally cannot be changed without a vote of a majority of the outstanding voting securities of the fund.

The prospectus, statement of additional information, annual reports, and semiannual reports provide you with explanations about portfolio terms, sales charges, risks, investment objectives, organizational structure, and many other important considerations (see Chapter 4). Become familiar with these informational pieces and you will better understand investing and mutual funds in particular.

Managing the Fund's Portfolio

A mutual fund's prospectus states the *fundamental policies* of the fund: those procedures designed to achieve the fund's investment objective. The fund's investment objective itself is a fundamental policy. Securities that may be purchased and the investment restrictions are also fundamental policies. The investment discipline for managing the portfolio may not be a fundamental policy unless so stated in the prospectus or statement of additional information.

The performance of the fund may suffer due to the adverse market conditions of the specified market in which the fund invests. However, the fund's investment objective precludes the portfolio manager from investing in markets contrary to its fundamental policies. For instance, if foreign stocks are performing poorly and United States stocks are performing well, the manager of an international stock fund could not arbitrarily decide to purchase United States stocks to improve fund performance. Of course, the fund's portfolio manager is always attempting to achieve positive returns for the fund and meet the fund's objective.

Mutual Fund Management Company

The mutual fund management company is operated by the board of directors or trustees and its officers. The management company employs the firm that serves as investment manager and other support organizations. Many times the mutual fund management company serves as the investment manager.

Board of Directors or Trustees

The board of directors or trustees reviews the performance of the funds and services being rendered to the shareholders, reviews distributions to the shareholders, and ensures the mutual fund is being operated under applicable federal and state regulations.

Officers

The fund's officers (president, secretary, treasurer, etc.) manage the fund's daily administrative and business activities.

Investment Manager

The mutual fund's investment manager, also known as an *investment adviser*, provides the organizational structure for the management for the family of mutual funds. The investment manager serves the mutual fund as an adviser, manager, or administrator. Also, the investment manager manages the investments of the fund's assets, determines the asset allocation, and places the buy and sell orders for the portfolio's underlying securities. The investment manager usually hires a portfolio manager to manage the fund's assets.

Subadviser

Some investment managers hire another firm, known as a *subadviser*, to manage the fund's portfolio and provide investment advice. Subadvisers are used many times when the investment manager is offering an international or special type of mutual fund. The portfolio manager, who manages the underlying securities on a daily basis, normally is employed by the subadviser.

Portfolio Manager

The portfolio manager is the individual or individuals responsible for the daily management of the mutual fund's portfolio such as deciding the quantity, price, and time to buy or sell specific securities for the portfolio. The portfolio manager is charged to buy only securities that he or she believes meet the investment objective requirements as set forth in the mutual fund's prospectus.

The portfolio manager(s) may be:

- an individual
- A team
- A committee
- Multiple portfolio managers
- Other type of organization

Furthermore, the portfolio manager usually has a staff of research analysts, computer technicians, and traders. The manager typically reviews the fund's portfolio daily and in most cases periodically throughout the day.

Portfolio of Underlying Securities

The prospectus defines which type of securities and in which industries the fund will invest to meet its investment objective. Usually, the prospectus states a percent of the fund's total assets will be invested in certain types of securities. For example, 70 percent of the fund's total assets will be invested in common stocks that have a record of paying dividends and, in the opinion of the investment manager, have the potential for increasing dividends. Thus, the other 30 percent of the total assets may be invested in other types of securities.

Three other examples of portfolios' compositions from varying funds are:

1. The fund may invest up to 35 percent of its total assets in securities issued by foreign entities.
2. The fund must invest at least 75 percent of its total assets in municipal bonds rated investment grade (BBB or higher by Standard & Poor's or Baa or higher by Moody's).

3. The fund must invest at least 65 percent of its total assets in the equities securities of health science companies throughout the world.

Investment Restrictions

Besides knowing what the mutual fund must invest in, the prospectus will also state what the fund is not allowed to invest in. For example, the fund may *not*

- invest more than 5 percent of the value of its total assets in the securities of any one issuer.
- purchase more than 10 percent of all outstanding voting securities or more than 10 percent of any class of securities of any one issuer.
- invest 25 percent or more of the value of its total assets in securities in any one industry.
- invest in certain types of mortgage-backed securities, such as interest-only stripped mortgage-backed securities, principal-only stripped mortgage-backed securities, and inverse floating rate collateralized mortgage obligations.

Other investment restrictions may state:

- The fund may not invest more than 20 percent of the total value of the fund's assets in tax-exempt securities that are not rated.
- The fund may not invest more than 15 percent of the fund's total assets in bonds rated below investment grade.
- The fund may not invest more than 10 percent of the fund's total assets in illiquid securities.
- The fund may not purchase securities on margin (borrow against the securities).

Currency Management Strategies

When the fund invests in foreign securities, it may use several techniques (called hedging) to reduce the risk of currency changes against the U.S. dollar or other currencies. *Hedging* attempts to reduce risk by buying or selling a different security (or contract) than the security (or contract) which is being traded. Three of the techniques used as a hedge against fluctuations in foreign currency exchange rates are trading:

1. Forward foreign currency exchange contracts
2. Options contracts on foreign currencies
3. Futures contracts on foreign currencies

The portfolio manager of a fund that owns foreign stocks and bonds has three choices regarding currency management:

1. Do not hedge.
2. Hedge the total portfolio.
3. Hedge a portion of the portfolio.

The prospectus may dictate to what extent the portfolio manager may strive to hedge the portfolio of foreign securities.

Do not hedge. Many international portfolio managers do not hedge the portfolio for currency risk at all. They may believe that a correlation exists between the foreign equity markets and its currency. If the manager likes the equity market, then he or she likes the currency. Other portfolio managers believe that currency fluctuations tend to smooth out over an extended period of time. One reason people invest in international funds is to diversify their assets; thus those investors want to own investments denominated in foreign currency. Hedging the currency risk in a mutual fund eliminates this objective. Another disadvantage is that hedging the currency risk may eliminate some or all of the investment return.

Hedge the total portfolio. Hedging the total portfolio basically eliminates most of the currency risk. The returns derived from the underlying securities are only market related. An advantage from hedging the entire portfolio is reducing the volatility of the underlying securities from currency exchange movements. A disadvantage in hedging the entire portfolio is the costs associated with hedging. The costs can be significant and cause a reduction in the investment returns.

Hedge a portion of the portfolio. Hedging a portion of the portfolio reduces some of the currency risk but not entirely. If the hedging is successful, investment returns may be enhanced by an incremental amount, thus producing a better return than a comparable fund that does not hedge or one that hedges its entire portfolio. (*The Value Line Mutual Fund Advisor,* May 28, 1996.)

Currency hedging transactions may cause additional risks and costs to the portfolio. If the strategy is managed successfully in relation to the full portfolio, increased returns (or reduced risk) may occur. Read the prospectus to determine if the fund is allowed to employ these types of investment techniques and for further explanations. Also, read the annual reports to determine if in fact the fund is currently using these techniques and if it is meeting its investment objective(s). Refer to Financial Focus 3 in Appendix B for more discussion about international economics.

Other Investment Techniques

In an effort to increase total return, some funds may employ various investment techniques such as lending portfolio securities, trading options and futures, and short-selling securities. These types of transactions may cause additional risks to the portfolio, but if properly executed also may increase returns. Read the prospectus for further explanations to determine if the fund is allowed to employ these types of investment techniques and also read the annual reports to determine if in fact the fund is currently using these techniques and meeting its investment objective(s).

Portfolio Turnover Rate

Portfolio turnover rate describes how often the portfolio's securities are bought and sold during the year. Higher portfolio turnover rates usually cause additional brokerage commissions and expenses. Also, higher portfolio turnover rates may generate more net realized short-term gains that are taxable to shareholders as ordinary income. Some funds' policies limit the amount of the portfolio turnover rate.

Operational Organizations

In addition to operating a management company and managing the mutual fund's assets, several organizations are needed to process the business and maintain proper controls. A custodian, transfer agent, dividend disbursing agent, and independent accountants are other organizations employed by the management company.

Custodian

A custodian, typically a bank or trust company, is responsible for the safekeeping of certificates and performing account information services.

Transfer Agent

A transfer agent, typically a bank or trust company, is responsible for maintaining the shareholders' accounts, issuing new certificates when shares are purchased, and canceling certificates when shares are sold. Transfer agents also are responsible for reregistering the name on the certificate when they receive proper instructions to do so. Reregistering means changing ownership of the funds' shares.

Dividend Disbursing Agent

A dividend disbursing agent, typically a bank or trust company, is responsible for paying the dividends and capital gains distributions to the appropriate shareholders. Many mutual funds pay dividends and distributions in additional shares and automatically credit the shareholder's account unless the shareholder requests that dividends and/or distributions be paid in cash. Only shareholders of record for a particular distribution are entitled to receive that distribution. A *shareholder of record* means that person who owns the shares of the mutual fund as of a certain date. The mutual fund board of directors or trustees review dividends and capital gains distributions to be paid to shareholders of record as of a specific date.

Many mutual fund management companies use the same bank, trust department, or other service company to do all three functions of custodian, transfer agent, and dividend disbursing agent. In some cases, the mutual fund management company establishes its own subsidiaries to do these functions.

Independent Accountant

A certified public accountant, independent of the fund, is responsible for preparing the fund's tax returns and auditing the mutual fund's financial operations. The accountant also determines the tax status of the mutual fund's distributions paid to the shareholders.

CHAPTER 7

Understanding Indexes, Averages, and Benchmarks

Many companies calculate and provide stock, bond, and mutual fund indexes and averages for investors to use for performance comparisons and to follow the markets. Indexes (also known as *indices*) and averages are used to measure and report value changes in representative stock, bond, and mutual fund groupings. Strictly speaking, an average is simply the arithmetic mean of a group of prices, whereas an index is an average expressed in relation to an earlier established base market value (Source: *Barron's Finance & Investment Handbook*). Indexes or averages are usually measured against a *benchmark*—a number that is fixed when the index or average is originally established.

Characteristics of a Valid Index or Average

Total return calculations of indexes and averages have become increasingly important. Both the performance measurement standards set by the Association for Investment Management and Research (AIMR) and the executive compensation ruling by the Securities and Exchange Commission (SEC) require total return performance calculations and comparison to appropriate market benchmarks. AIMR is a firm that specializes in standardizing and calculating investment performance returns. (Source: *S&P 500 1996 Directory.*)

Salomon Brothers' philosophy states that an index or average is considered a good benchmark if it has the following six characteristics:

1. It is relevant to investors.
2. It is comprehensive to include all opportunities that are available to investors.
3. It includes objective criteria to determine which securities are included during a particular day.
4. It is replicable by investors so that they may follow it over time as a strategy.
5. It is stable in that the components do not change very often.
6. It is easily understood for determining the criteria of inclusion for the components. (Source: *Salomon Brothers Global Index Catalog.*)

Indexes and averages do not reflect sales charges, fees, or expenses; investing in mutual funds and other securities entails fees and expenses. These indexes and averages help you compare the performances of different funds by putting them on equal footing. It's like comparing fractions by converting them to a common denominator.

Market-value-capitalization-weighted. Most stock indexes or averages use market-value-capitalization weightings when calculating the index or average value. The *market value capitalization* (also known as *market capitalization*) of a stock is calculated by multiplying its price per share by the number of shares outstanding. For example, XYZ Company stock price is $75 with 2,000,000 shares outstanding. The market value capitalization is $150 million ($75 times 2,000,000). The sum of the market value capitalization of the individual companies which comprise the index or average is the aggregate market value which is then indexed, or expressed in relation, to a base period market value. Each stock's weight in the index or average is proportionate to its market value capitalization.

Price-weighted. Some stock indexes and averages use price weightings when calculating the index or average value. The index or average is calculated by adding the prices of the stocks in the index or average and dividing the sum by an index or average divisor. The index or average divisor is a factor that adjusts for stock splits over the years.

Equal-weighted. Most mutual fund indexes and averages are calculated by giving each fund equal weighting in the index or average. Equal weightings prevent one or two large-size funds from dominating the index or average returns.

Points, not dollars. Averages and indexes are usually quoted in points and not dollars. A point is a unit used in quoting averages, indexes, and sometimes prices of securities.

Adjustments. Every change in stock, bond, or mutual fund price for either an index or average must be adjusted to eliminate the influences of corporate actions (such as a stock split) so that the index or average reflects only movements resulting from market activity.

Recalculation of an index or average. Indexes or averages may be reconstituted periodically to reflect changes in the marketplace. *Reconstitution,* also known as *recalculation* or *rebalancing,* means that the values and financial data of securities in the index or average are tabulated again and are reclassified based on the methodology of the index or average, if necessary.

Index performance. Index performance can be measured as a percentage change of an index for a given period of time, excluding any income earned from the underlying securities. However, the *index total return* includes any income earned from the underlying securities, plus the percentage change of the index for a given period of time. The income can be indexed using the same method used in calculating the index and can be assumed to be reinvested (such as daily, monthly, quarterly, or semiannually, depending on the type and calculation method of the index). Some indexes provide both the index return and index total return; other indexes provide only one. When analyzing indexes, know whether the index performance is just for the index return (includes only price change) or for the index total return (includes price change and income earned).

Limitations

Investors cannot invest directly in an index or average. The index or average does not reflect any fees or expenses. When comparing the performance of a stock or bond index or average to the performance of a mutual fund, the securities that comprise an index or average are not necessarily representative of a fund's composition.

You should understand mutual fund, bond, and stock indexes and averages to measure performance of bond and stock mutual funds.

Mutual Fund Indexes and Averages

Several mutual fund research firms publish mutual fund indexes and averages. Three top companies are CDA/Wiesenberger; IBC Financial Data, Inc.; and Lipper Analytical Services, Inc.

CDA/Wiesenberger

CDA/Wiesenberger publishes broad mutual fund performance indexes for growth, growth/income, balanced, and income. They also publish approximately 30 mutual fund classification indexes. (Source: CDA/Wiesenberger.)

IBC Financial Data, Inc.

IBC Financial Data, Inc. publishes *IBC's Money Fund Report.* Published weekly for 7-day, 30-day, and one-year simple and compound (assumes reinvested dividends) yields, the average represents all major money market mutual fund yields (no criteria for inclusion in average). (Source: IBC Financial Data, Inc.)

FIGURE 7.1   Lipper Mutual Fund Index Categories

Equity

Balanced Funds Index	Capital Appreciation Funds Index
Convertible Securities Funds Index	Emerging Markets
Equity Income Funds Index	European Region Funds Index
Financial Services Funds Index	Flexible Portfolio Funds Index
Global Flexible Portfolio Funds Index	Global Funds Index
Gold Oriented Funds Index	Growth and Income Funds Index
Growth Funds Index	Health/Biotechnology Funds Index
International Funds Index	MidCap Funds Index
Pacific Region Funds Index	S&P 500 Index Objective Funds Index
Science and Technology Funds Index	Small Company Growth Funds Index
Utility Funds Index	

Taxable Fixed Income

Adjustable Rate Mortgage Funds Index	Corporate Debt Funds A Rated Index
Corporate Debt Funds BBB Rated Index	Flexible Income Funds Index
General Bond Funds Index	General U.S. Government Funds Index
General U.S. Treasury Funds Index	General World Income Funds Index
GNMA Funds Index	High Current Yield Funds Index
Intermediate Investment Grade Debt Funds Index	Intermediate U.S. Government Funds Index
Money Market Funds Index	Short Intermediate Investment Grade Debt Funds Index
Short Intermediate U.S. Government Funds Index	Short Investment Grade Debt Funds Index
Short U.S. Government Funds Index	U.S. Mortgage Funds Index

Tax-Exempt Fixed Income

General Municipal Debt Funds Index	High Yield Municipal Debt Funds Index
Insured Municipal Debt Funds Index	Intermediate Municipal Debt Funds Index
Short Intermediate Municipal Debt Funds Index	Short Municipal Debt Funds Index
Tax-exempt Money Market Funds Index	California Intermediate Municipal Debt Funds

FIGURE 7.1   Lipper Mutual Fund Index Categories (Continued)

Tax-Exempt Fixed Income (continued)

Florida Municipal Debt Funds IndexCalifornia Municipal Debt Funds Index	Massachusetts Municipal Debt Funds Index
Maryland Municipal Debt Funds Index	Minnesota Municipal Debt Funds Index
Michigan Municipal Debt Funds Index	New York State Municipal Debt Funds Index
New Jersey Municipal Debt Funds Index	Ohio Municipal Debt Funds Index
Virginia Municipal Debt Funds Index	Pennsylvania Municipal Debt Funds Index

---

Lipper Analytical Services, Inc.

Lipper Analytical Services, Inc. provides performance indexes for equity, taxable fixed income, and tax-exempt fixed income mutual funds. Each category is comprised of appropriate indexes. Comparing a mutual fund's performance to the Lipper Indexes is the industry standard. Figure 7.1 shows Lipper Analytical Services index categories. (Source: Lipper Analytical Services, Inc.)

Locating Mutual Fund Indexes and Averages

Several firms publish mutual fund indexes and averages for different classifications of funds: domestic, international, and global markets. The indexes and averages are reported by research firms and by periodicals, or ask your investment professional for the index values and information.

Many mutual fund indexes and averages are also quoted in the *Wall Street Journal, Barron's, Investor's Business Daily,* and *USA Today.* The well-known indexes and averages are reported also in local newspapers, in magazines, and on the World Wide Web. Figure 7.2 shows where you may find mutual fund indexes and averages in newspapers.

FIGURE 7.2   Locating Mutual Fund Indexes and Averages

Periodical	Place and Heading
The Wall Street Journal	Section C: "Lipper Indexes"

Barron's	Market Week:
	    "Lipper Mutual Fund Performance Averages"
	    "Lipper Mutual Fund Performance Indexes"
	    "Money Market Funds"

Investor's Business Daily *USA Today*	Section B Section B "USA Today's Market Scoreboard"

Bond Indexes and Averages

Many firms publish bond indexes and averages for groups of bonds, industries, and marketplaces for domestic, international, and global markets.

Locating Bond Indexes and Averages

The bond indexes and averages are reported by research firms, brokerage firms who publish them, and by periodicals; or ask your investment professional for the index values and information. Many of the bond indexes and averages are also quoted in the *Wall Street Journal, Barron's, Investor's Business Daily,* and *USA Today.* The well-known indexes and averages are reported also in local newspapers, in magazines, and on the World Wide Web. Figure 7.3 shows where you may find bond indexes and averages in newspapers.

Total Return of Indexes

Many bond indexes and averages, such as the Lehman Brothers bond indexes, define total return as the price appreciation or depreciation on an investment, plus any income received, expressed as a per-

FIGURE 7.3 Locating Bond Indexes and Averages

Periodical	Place and Heading

The Wall Street Journal	Section C:
	    "Markets Diary"
	    "Bond Market Data Bank"

Barron's	Market Week: "Barron's Market Laboratory-Bonds"
Investor's Business Daily	Section B
USA Today	Section B "USA Today's Market Scoreboard"

centage of the initial investment, inclusive of accrued interest paid. The standard components of total return for the indexes are price and coupon return. The coupon return is the coupon rate (interest rate) stated on the bond times the bond's par value (generally $1,000). For holding periods greater than one month, coupon return also includes a reinvestment component. All cash flows received are reinvested monthly in market-value-weighted proportion across all securities that currently qualify for inclusion in the index.

Dow Jones & Co. Bond Averages

Dow Jones & Company, Inc., is the most recognized name worldwide for publishing and providing financial information.

Dow Jones 20 Bond Average. The Dow Jones 20 Bond Average represents the average of the averages of two groups of bonds: ten public utility bonds and ten industrial bonds.

Lehman Brothers Bond Indexes

Lehman Brothers Inc. is a major financial services firm both domestically and internationally. The firm is considered a premier company for trading fixed-income securities, investment banking, and providing fixed-income indexes for the debt market. Approximately two-thirds of the institutional fixed-income portfolio managers follow Lehman Brothers indexes.

The investment-grade indexes provided by Lehman Brothers consist of debt securities with maturities of one year and longer, and a minimum outstanding par value of $100 million. Although an index may be compiled for any range or length of maturity, the standard maturity range is the intermediate, which is from 1 year to 9.99 years, and the long-term, which is 10 years or longer. Other indexes are created for different types of industry groups, market sectors, and credit quality. (Source: Lehman Brothers Inc.)

Lehman Brothers Aggregate Bond Index. This index consists of the Lehman Brothers Government Bond Index, Lehman Brothers Corporate Bond Index, Lehman Brothers Mortgage-Backed Securities Index, and Lehman Brothers Asset-Backed Securities Index.

Lehman Brothers Government Bond Index. This index consists of the Lehman Brothers Treasury Bond Index and the Lehman Brothers Agency Bond Index.

Lehman Brothers Treasury Bond Index. This index contains all public obligations of the U.S. Treasury, excluding flower bonds and foreign-targeted issues.

Lehman Brothers Agency Bond Index. This index is composed of all publicly issued debt of U.S. federal agencies, quasi-federal corporations, and corporate debt guaranteed by the U.S. government.

Lehman Brothers Corporate Bond Index. This index includes all publicly issued, fixed-rate, dollar-denominated, investment-grade, nonconvertible, SEC-registered corporate debt.

Lehman Brothers Mortgage-Backed Securities Index. This index includes fixed-rate securities backed by 30-year and 15-year, and balloon payment mortgage pools of the Government National Mortgage Association (GNMA), Federal Home Loan Mortgage Corporation (FHLMC), and Federal National Mortgage Association (FNMA).

Lehman Brothers Asset-Backed Securities Index. This index is composed of credit card, automobile, and home equity loans that have an average life of at least one year.

Lehman Brothers Intermediate Government/Corporate Index. This index is composed of investment-grade corporate and government bonds with maturities between 1 and 9.99 years.

Lehman Brothers Long Government/Corporate Index. This index is composed of investment-grade corporate and government bonds with maturities of 10 years or longer.

Lehman Brothers 1–3 Year Government Index. This index is composed of all publicly issued debt of the U.S. Treasury, federal agencies, quasi-federal corporations, and corporate debt guaranteed by the U.S. government with maturities of one to three years.

Lehman Brothers 20+ Treasury Index. This index is composed of all public obligations of the U.S. Treasury with maturities of 20 years or longer.

Lehman Brothers High Yield Index. This index is composed of dollar-denominated, noninvestment-grade, nonconvertible, SEC-registered corporate bonds with maturities of one year or longer. The index includes only noninvestment-grade bonds (i.e., bonds rated Ba1 and BB+ or lower by Moody's and S&P, respectively).

Lehman Brothers Municipal Bond Index. This index consists of investment-grade tax-exempt bonds of deals of originally $50 million or larger that have an outstanding par value greater than $3 million with a remaining maturity of at least one year.

Merrill Lynch Bond Indexes

Merrill Lynch & Company, Inc. is a leading securities brokerage, investment banking, and financial services firm both domestically and internationally. (Reprinted by permission of Merrill Lynch, Pierce,

Fenner & Smith Incorporated. Copyright Merrill Lynch, Pierce, Fenner & Smith Incorporated.)

Merrill Lynch Corporate Master Index. This index is a market-capitalization-weighted index including fixed-coupon domestic investment-grade corporate bonds with at least $100 million par amount outstanding. Quality range of the issues is rated BBB– to AAA by S&P and Baa3 to Aaa by Moody's.

Merrill Lynch Corporate 1–9.99 Year Index. This index is a market-capitalization-weighted index including fixed-coupon domestic-grade corporate bonds with at least $100 million par amount outstanding. Maturities for all bonds are 1 to 9.99 years. Quality range of the issues is Baa3 to Aaa rated by Moody's and BBB– to AAA rated by S&P.

Merrill Lynch Corporate 10+ Year Index. This index is a market-capitalization-weighted index including fixed-coupon domestic-grade corporate bonds with at least $100 million par amount outstanding. Maturities for all bonds are ten years or longer. Quality range of the issues is Baa3 to Aaa rated by Moody's and BBB– to AAA rated by S&P.

Merrill Lynch Domestic Master Index. This index is a market-capitalization-weighted index including fixed-coupon domestic-grade corporate, government and mortgage pass-through bonds. Maturities for all bonds are greater or equal to one year. Quality range of the issues is rated BBB– to Treasury quality by S&P and Baa3 to Treasury quality by Moody's.

Merrill Lynch GNMA Master Index. This index is a market-capitalization-weighted index including generic-coupon GNMA mortgages with at least $100 million par amount outstanding. Generic pass-through securities are composed of numerous mortgage pools with various maturities.

Merrill Lynch Global Bond Index. This index is a market-capitalization-weighted index including international and domestic government and corporate bonds.

Salomon Brothers Bond Indexes

Salomon Brothers, Inc. is a major financial services firm both domestically and internationally. The firm is considered a premier company for trading fixed-income securities. (Source: © Salomon Brothers Inc. All rights reserved.)

Salomon Brothers Broad Investment-Grade (BIG) Bond Index[SM]. This index is market-capitalization-weighted and includes treasury, government-sponsored, mortgage, and investment-grade fixed-rate corporate issues with a maturity of one year or longer, and a minimum amount outstanding of $1 billion for treasuries and mortgages and $100 million for corporate and government-sponsored issues.

Salomon Brothers High-Grade Corporate Index[SM]. This index includes those issues from the Corporate Index that have at least ten years to maturity (long-term) and a minimum credit rating of Aa3 by Moody's and AA– by S&P.

Salomon Brothers World Government Bond Index[SM]. This index is a market-capitalization-weighted benchmark that tracks the performance of the 17 government bonds markets of Australia, Austria, Belgium, Canada, Denmark, Finland, France, Germany, Ireland, Italy, Japan, the Netherlands, Spain, Sweden, Switzerland, the United Kingdom, and the United States.

Salomon Brothers Non-U.S. Dollar World Government Bond Index[SM]. This index is a market-capitalization-weighted benchmark that tracks the performance of the government bonds markets of the Salomon Brothers World Government Bond Index, excluding the United States.

Credit Suisse First Boston Indexes

Credit Suisse First Boston is a major financial services firm both domestically and internationally. The firm is considered a premier company for underwriting new issues and mergers and acquisitions. (Source: Credit Suisse First Boston.)

Credit Suisse First Boston High Yield Index. The Credit Suisse First Boston High Yield Index is the industry benchmark most widely used by fund managers to gauge performance. The index has an inception date of January 1986 and is one of only a few indexes that provides extensive historical data. Reflecting the changing needs of the high-yield market, index data became available on a weekly basis in January 1994. Items including returns, average price, yield, spread-to-treasury, and duration are all available.

The index is an unmanaged, trader-priced portfolio constructed to mirror the high-yield debt market. The index can be subdivided to isolate data for specific sectors of the high-yield market, including cash pay, zerofix, pay-in-kind, and defaulted sectors, or modules. The modular nature of the index allows customization of data to meet investors' needs. Modules that are commonly used include industry, market value, seniority, yield, and credit rating. The index is divided into three tiers by credit rating based on both Moody's and S&P ratings:

1. Upper tier: Split BBB issues (issues with one Baa or BBB and one Ba or BB rating), BB issues and split BB issues (issues with one Ba or BB and one B rating).
2. Middle tier: Single B issues and split single B issues (issues with one B and one Caa or CCC rating).
3. Lower tier: All issues rated Caa or CCC and below, including defaulted securities.

The Bond Buyer Municipal Bond Indexes

The Bond Buyer publishes *The Bond Buyer,* which reviews and reports information about the municipal bond market and municipal bond issuers. (Source: The Bond Buyer.)

Bond Buyer Municipal Index. This index contains 40 long-term municipal bonds. The index is calculated twice a day, at noon and 3:00 P.M. EST. The index value is based on price quotations provided by municipal bond dealer-to-dealer brokers. The composition of the index is revised twice a month, on the 15th and the last business day of the month. Revision adds newly issued municipal bonds to the index and drops the least actively traded bonds.

FIGURE 7.4   Locating Stock Indexes and Averages

Periodical	Place and Heading
The Wall Street Journal	Section C:
	"Markets Diary"
	"Stock Market Data Bank"
	"Dow Jones Global Indexes"
	"Stock Market Indexes"
Barron's	Market Week:
	"Barron's Market Laboratory-Stocks"
Investor's Business Daily	Section A
USA Today	Section B
	"USA Today's Market Scoreboard"

20-Bond Buyer Index. This index consists of 20 general obligation bonds that mature in 20 years. It is calculated once a week on Thursday. The average rating of the 20 bonds is roughly equivalent to Moody's Aa3 rating and S&P AA– rating.

11-Bond Buyer Index. This index uses a select group of 11 bonds in the 20-Bond Index. It is calculated once a week on Thursday. The average rating of the 11 bonds is roughly equivalent to Moody's Aa1 and S&P AA+.

Revenue Bond Index. This index consists of 25 various revenue bonds that mature in 30 years. It is calculated once a week on Thursday. The average rating is roughly equivalent to Moody's A1 and S&P A+.

Stock Indexes and Averages

Many research and brokerage firms publish stock indexes and averages for groups of stocks, industries, and marketplaces for domestic, international, and global markets.

Locating Stock Indexes and Averages

The indexes and averages are reported by research firms, brokerage firms who publish them, and by periodicals; or you can ask your investment professional for the index values and information. Many stock indexes and averages are also quoted in the *Wall Street Journal, Barron's, Investor's Business Daily,* and *USA Today.* The well-known indexes and averages are reported also in local newspapers, in magazines, and on the World Wide Web. Figure 7.4 shows where you may find stock indexes and averages in newspapers.

Calculating Indexes and Averages

Most indexes and averages are calculated using a market-capitalization, base-weighted methodology. The *base period* is the date on which the index is first calculated. The *base period market value* is the total market value of all of the companies in the index. A company's *market value,* using the market-capitalization method, is calculated by multiplying the shares outstanding by the market price of the stock. The *index base period market value (index value)* is set at the time of the base period. The *base period index divisor* is the total market value of the index divided by the index value. The index divisor is adjusted to reflect any companies added or removed from the index, change of shares outstanding, a company spin-off, and other corporate actions. The index is calculated by dividing the total market value of all stocks in the index by the latest index divisor.

Total Return of Indexes. *Total return* of many stock indexes, such as the Standard & Poor's 500 Total Return Index, is calculated by adding the indexed dividend income to the Index price change for a given period of time. The *indexed dividend* is an index number that represents the dividend distributions of the companies in the index. To calculate the indexed dividend, add the total daily dividends (based on the ex-dividend date) for all of the stocks in the index for a given time period and then convert that sum to an indexed number by dividing it by the same index divisor that is used to calculate the actual index. The index price change is calculated by subtracting the closing value of the index for that period from the closing value of the index at the beginning of the time period. (Source: *S&P 500 1996 Directory.*)

Dow Jones & Co. Stock Indexes and Averages

Dow Jones & Company, Inc., is the most recognized name worldwide for publishing and providing financial information and stock indexes and averages. Dow Jones & Company publishes the *Wall Street Journal, Barron's,* and several other national and international newspapers. Dow Jones & Company also electronically provides the worldwide *Dow Jones News Service* and the *Wall Street Journal* interactive edition (http://www.wsj.com).

Dow Jones Industrial Average. The Dow Jones Industrial Average (DJIA), generally referred as the "Dow" or the "industrials," is the most recognized and publicized stock market average or index. The DJIA represents 30 well-known companies. The Dow, a price-weighted average, is computed by adding the stock prices of the 30 companies and dividing by a factor that adjusts for stock splits over the years. The average is quoted in points, not dollars.

Dow Jones Utility Average. The Dow Jones Utility Average, a price-weighted average, represents 15 well-established gas and electric power companies.

Dow Jones Transportation Average. The Dow Jones Transportation Average, a price-weighted average, represents 20 airlines, railroads, and trucking companies.

Dow Jones 65 Composite Average. The Dow Jones 65 Composite Average represents all 65 companies included in the Dow Jones Industrial Average, Dow Jones Utility Average, and Dow Jones Transportation Average.

Dow Jones World Stock Index. This index represents performance results from more than a dozen countries grouped in three geographic regions: the Americas, Europe, and Asia/Pacific. The index measures the movement of stocks of more than 2,700 companies.

Dow Jones World Stock Index. (ex. U.S.) This index represents performance results from more than a dozen countries grouped in three geographic regions: the Americas, Europe, and Asia/Pacific, excluding the United States Equity Market Index.

Standard & Poor's Stock Indexes

Standard & Poor's (S&P) is a leader in providing credit ratings and research information for the securities markets to both investors and financial service firms. S&P publishes numerous reports and books about the performance, financial data, and ratings for mutual funds, stocks, bonds, and money market securities. S&P indexes represent stocks from 118 industry groups across 11 economic sectors. (Source: Standard & Poor's.)

Standard & Poor's 500 Index. This index consists of 500 stocks chosen for market capitalization, liquidity, and industry group representation. Specifically, the companies are chosen for the index because they are leading companies in leading industries. The S&P 500 Index, a market-capitalization-weighted index, is one of the most widely used indexes of United States stock market performance.

The S&P 500 Index is comprised of the S&P 400 Industrial Index, S&P 40 Utilities Index, S&P 20 Transportation Index, and S&P 40 Financial Index.

Standard & Poor's 400 Industrial Index. This index is market-capitalization-weighted and represents 400 large well-established industrial companies.

Standard & Poor's 40 Utilities Index. This index is market-capitalization weighted and represents 40 well-established gas and electric power companies.

Standard & Poor's 20 Transportation Index. This index is a market-capitalization-weighted index and represents 20 airlines, railroads, and trucking companies.

Standard & Poor's 40 Financial Index. This index is a market-capitalization-weighted index and represents 40 banks and other financial services companies.

Standard & Poor's 400 MidCap Index. This index consists of 400 domestic stocks chosen for market capitalization, liquidity, and industry group representation. The index is market-capitalization-weighted, with each stock's weight in the index proportionate to its market capitalization. The stocks represented in the index have market capitalizations between approximately $800 million and $3 billion.

Standard & Poor's 600 SmallCap Index. This index consists of 600 domestic stocks chosen for market capitalization ranging from the 50th to 83rd percentile of the stocks listed on the NYSE, AMEX, or the Nasdaq Stock Market. Real estate investment trusts (REITs), limited partnerships, closed-end funds, royalty trusts, and foreign securities that trade as American Depositary Receipts are excluded from the index. Other criteria include trading activity, stock price (must be $1 or more), and financial condition. The index is market-capitalization-weighted, with each stock's weight in the index proportionate to its market capitalization.

Standard & Poor's 1500 Supercomposite. This index is the combination of the S&P 500 Index, S&P MidCap 400 Index, and the S&P SmallCap 600 Index. It represents approximately 97 percent of the institutionally investable domestic equity universe.

Standard & Poor's and BARRA Indexes

In May 1992, Standard & Poor's and BARRA, an investment technology firm, released the S&P 500/BARRA Value Index and the S&P 500/BARRA Growth Index. These two indexes split the S&P 500 Index into two mutually exclusive groups designed to track two of the predominant investment styles in the U.S. equity market. The S&P 500/BARRA Value Index and S&P 500/BARRA Growth Index are constructed by separating the stocks in the S&P 500 Index according to a single attribute: price-book ratio. *Price* means the market price per share of the stock. *Book* means the book value per share of the company. Approximately 50 percent of the S&P 500 Index capitalization is represented in the S&P 500/BARRA Value Index and 50 percent in the S&P 500/BARRA Growth Index. (Source: Standard & Poor's.)

S&P 500/BARRA Value Index. This index consists of stocks that also have lower price-earnings ratios, higher dividend yields, and lower historical and predicted earnings growth, in addition to lower price-book ratios.

S&P 500/BARRA Growth Index. This index consists of stocks that also have higher price-earnings ratios, lower dividend yields, higher predicted earnings growth, and larger capital market capitalizations, in addition to higher price-book ratios.

Additionally, Standard & Poor's and BARRA created two other indexes from the S&P MidCap 400 Index: S&P MidCap 400/BARRA Value Index and S&P MidCap 400/BARRA Growth Index. The S&P MidCap 400/BARRA Value Index and S&P MidCap 400/BARRA Growth Index are constructed by separating the stocks in the S&P MidCap 400 Index according to a single attribute: price-book ratio. Approximately 50 percent of the S&P MidCap 400 Index capitalization is represented in the S&P MidCap 400/BARRA Value Index and 50 percent in the S&P MidCap 400/BARRA Growth Index.

S&P MidCap 400/BARRA Value Index. This index consists of stocks that have lower price-earnings ratios and lower historical and predicted earnings growth, in addition to lower price-book ratios.

S&P MidCap 400/BARRA Growth Index. This index consists of stocks that have higher price-earnings ratios, higher predicted earnings growth, and larger capital market capitalizations, in addition to higher price-book ratios.

New York Stock Exchange Common Stock Indexes

New York Stock Exchange Composite Index. This index is a measure of the changes in aggregate market value of the New York Stock Exchange (NYSE) common stocks, adjusted to eliminate the effects of capitalization changes, new listings, and delistings. The base market value was purposely set at $50, because this figure was reasonably close to the actual average price of all common stocks on the base date of December 31, 1965.

The NYSE Composite Index consists of all common stocks listed on the New York Stock Exchange and four subgroup indexes (Source: New York Stock Exchange):

1. Industrial
2. Transportation
3. Utility
4. Finance

The Nasdaq Stock Market Indexes

Nasdaq Composite Index. This index is comprised of all issues listed on the Nasdaq Stock Market except for rights, warrants, units, and convertible debentures. The Composite Index is market-value weighted. Every security assigned to the Composite Index is also assigned to one of Nasdaq's eight other main indexes. These indexes are industrial, insurance, bank, other finance, transportation, telecommunications, computer, and biotechnology.

The Composite Index includes both Nasdaq National Market and Nasdaq Small-Cap Market domestic and foreign issues. The listing requirements for the Nasdaq National Market (NNM) are more stringent than for the Nasdaq Small-Cap Market, such as the number of shareholders, minimum bid price, market value of shares outstanding, number of shares outstanding, and assets. (Source: National Association of Securities Dealers, Inc.)

Nasdaq 100 Index. This index includes 100 of the largest nonfinancial domestic companies listed on the Nasdaq National Market tier of the Nasdaq Stock Market. Each security is proportionately represented by its market-capitalization in relation to the total market value of the index. This index reflects Nasdaq's largest growth companies across major industry groups. All index components have a minimum market capitalization of $500 million, and an average daily trading volume of at least 100,000 shares.

NNM Composite Index. This index is comprised of all issues listed on the Nasdaq National Market tier for the Nasdaq Stock Market except for rights, warrants, units, and convertible debentures. The NNM Composite Index is market-value-weighted.

Nasdaq Small-Cap Index. This index is comprised of all issues listed on Nasdaq Small-Cap Market tier for the Nasdaq Stock Market except for rights, warrants, units, and convertible debentures. The Nasdaq Small-Cap Index is market-value-weighted.

American Stock Exchange (AMEX) Index

AMEX Composite Index. This index is a market-capitalization–weighted, price appreciation index. The AMEX Composite Index represents the aggregate value of the common shares or ADRs of all AMEX-listed companies, REITs, master limited partnerships, and closed-end investment issues. (Source: American Stock Exchange.)

Frank Russell Company Indexes

Frank Russell Company is a leading provider of performance measurement and consulting services to the financial industry. Many of its stock indexes are used regularly in comparing returns for mutual funds and other registered investment advisers. (Source: Frank Russell Company.)

Russell 3000 Index. This index is composed of the 3,000 largest U.S. companies, as determined by market capitalization. This index of securities represents approximately 98 percent of the investable U.S. equity market.

Russell 1000 Index. This index consists of the 1,000 largest companies in the Russell 3000 Index, representing 88 percent of the total market capitalization of the Russell 3000 Index. This is a large cap (market-oriented) index because it comprises the universe of stocks from which most active managers typically select. The Russell 1000 is very highly correlated with the Standard & Poor's 500 Index.

Russell 2000 Index. This index consists of the smallest 2,000 companies in the Russell 3000 Index, representing about 12 percent of the Russell 3000 Index total market capitalization. This small-cap index is widely regarded in the industry as the premier measure of small-cap stocks.

Russell Top 200 Index. This index consists of the largest 200 companies in the Russell 1000 Index, as ranked by total market capitalization. This large-cap index is appropriate when comparing the performance of "blue chip" stock funds.

Russell Midcap Index. This index consists of the smallest 800 companies in the Russell 1000 Index, as ranked by total market capitalization. The Russell Midcap Index accurately captures the medium-sized universe of securities.

Frank Russell Company also publishes *style indexes* for value and growth. For these indexes, companies are separately sorted and ranked by their price-book ratio and their (I/B/E/S) forecast of long-term growth mean to determine their relative ranking according to each variable. Therefore, each of the above mentioned Russell indexes are expanded to include the following style indexes: Russell 3000 Value Index, Russell 3000 Growth Index, Russell 1000 Value Index, Russell 1000 Growth Index, Russell 2000 Value Index, Russell 2000 Growth Index, Russell Midcap Value Index, Russell Midcap Growth Index, Russell Top 200 Value Index, and Russell Top 200 Growth Index.

Russell 3000 Value Index This index contains those Russell 1000 Index and Russell 2000 Index securities with less-than-average growth orientation.

Russell 3000 Growth Index. This index contains those Russell 1000 Index and Russell 2000 Index securities with greater-than-average growth orientation.

Russell 1000 Value Index. This index contains those Russell 1000 Index securities with less-than-average growth orientation. Companies in this index generally have lower price-book and price-earnings ratios, higher dividend yields, and lower forecasted growth values.

Russell 1000 Growth Index. This index contains those Russell 1000 Index securities with greater-than-average growth orientation. Companies in this index generally have higher price-to-book and price-to-earnings ratios, lower dividend yields, and higher forecasted growth values.

Russell 2000 Value Index. This index contains those Russell 2000 Index securities with less-than-average growth orientation. Companies in this index generally have lower price-book and price-earnings ratios.

Russell 2000 Growth Index. This index contains those Russell 2000 Index securities with greater-than-average growth orientation. Companies in this index generally have higher price-book and price-earnings ratios.

Russell Midcap Value Index. This index contains those Russell Midcap Index securities with less-than-average growth orientation.

Russell Midcap Growth Index. This index contains those Russell Midcap Index securities with greater-than-average growth orientation.

Frank Russell indexes are available on its home page at http://www.russell.com.

Wilshire Associates Stock Indexes

Wilshire Associates is a leading provider of performance measurement and consulting services to the financial industry. Wilshire's stock indexes are used regularly in comparing returns for mutual funds and other registered investment advisers. (Source: Wilshire Associates.)

Wilshire 5000 Equity Index. This index measures the performance of all United States headquartered equity securities with readily available price data. More than 7,000 market-capitalization-weighted stocks are used to calculate the index. The index measures the performance of all stocks rather than the performance of any particular market segment.

Wilshire 4500 Equity Index. This index is the Wilshire 5000 Equity Index securities with the companies in the Standard & Poor's 500 Index removed.

Wilshire also publishes six style indexes, such as the Large Company Value, Large Company Growth, Mid Cap Company Value, Mid Cap Company Growth, Small Company Value, and Small Company Growth. Key variables used by the value index include price-earnings ratio, price-book ratio, and dividend yield. Variables used for the growth index include sales growth, return on equity, and dividend payout.

Morgan Stanley Capital International Stock Indexes

Morgan Stanley Capital International is a major provider of global and international stock indexes and averages. (Source: Morgan Stanley Capital International.)

Morgan Stanley Capital International Europe, Australasia, Far East Index (MSCI EAFE). This index is a market-capitalization-weighted index representing more than 1,000 securities listed on the stock exchanges of the following countries: Australia, Austria, Belgium, Denmark, Finland, France, Germany, Hong Kong, Ireland, Italy, Japan, the Netherlands, New Zealand, Norway, Singapore, Malaysia, Spain, Sweden, Switzerland, and the United Kingdom.

Morgan Stanley Capital International Europe, Australasia, Far East (XJPN) Index (MSCI EAFE-XJPN). This index is the same as the MSCI EAFE index without the Japan component.

Morgan Stanley Capital International World Index. This index is a market-capitalization-weighted index representing more than 1,500 securities listed on the stock exchanges of the following countries: Australia, Austria, Belgium, Canada, Denmark, Finland, France, Germany, Hong Kong, Ireland, Italy, Japan, the Netherlands, New Zealand, Norway, Singapore, Malaysia, Spain, Sweden, Switzerland, the United Kingdom, and the United States.

International Stock Exchange Indexes

International investing is significant to allocating assets to diverse markets outside the United States stock market. Therefore, knowing the performance of international stocks is important in relation to the performance of international and global mutual funds. (Source: *World Stock Exchange Fact Book.*)

All Ordinaires Index (Hong Kong). This index, a market-value-capitalization-weighted index, is comprised of all listed stocks with the exception of stocks of overseas incorporated companies whose principal activities are carried out abroad, stocks which have been suspended for over one year, and stocks which are not traded in Hong Kong dollars.

ASX All Ordinaires Price Index (Australia). This index consists of the top stocks by market capitalization covering about 92 percent of domestic company aggregate market value.

DAX Index (Germany). This index consists of 30 blue chip stocks based on turnover, market capitalization, and early availability of opening prices.

FT-SE 100 Index (United Kingdom). This index is comprised of the 100 largest companies by market value capitalization. FT-SE represents the Financial Times-Stock Exchange.

Hang Seng Index (Hong Kong). This index, a market-value-capitalization-weighted index, is comprised of the 33 largest and most liquid stocks traded in Hong Kong.

Nikkei 225 Index (Japan). This index consists of 225 Japanese companies listed in the first section of the Tokyo Stock Exchange. This index is a price-weighted index which means that the price movement of each stock, in yen or dollars, is equally weighted regardless of market capitalization.

Paris CAC–40 Index (France). This index is comprised of 40 of the largest stocks, by capitalization and by liquidity, on the official list.

SES All-Singapore Index (Singapore). This index, a market-capitalization-weighted index, consists of all listed Singapore ordinary shares.

Toronto 300 Composite Index. This index, also known as the *TSE 300,* is comprised of the 300 largest companies by market capitalization that are traded on the Toronto Stock Exchange (TSE).

Other Benchmarks

Certificates of deposit (CDs)—90 day. The average represents the monthly return equivalents of yield averages of three-month CDs for the period being calculated.

Certificates of deposit—180 day. The average represents the monthly return equivalents of yield averages of six-month CDs for the period being calculated.

U.S. Treasury bill—one year. The one-year U.S. Treasury bill average is an average of the current one-year U.S. Treasury bill issues for the period being calculated.

U.S. Treasury bill—90 day. The 90-day U.S. Treasury bill average is an average of the current 90-day U.S. Treasury bill issues for the period being calculated.

Economic Indexes

Investors want their returns to at least keep pace with inflation. The condition of the economy affects money market securities, bonds, and stocks. Some of the key economic indexes, which may be used as economic indicators, are the Consumer Price Index, Gross Domestic Product, the Index of Leading Economic Indicators, Producer Price Index, and Unemployment Rate.

Consumer Price Index (CPI-U). The Consumer Price Index for All Urban Consumers is a measure of the average change in the prices of a fixed basket of goods and services paid by urban consumers, including food, transportation, shelter, utilities, clothing, medical care, entertainment, and other items. The CPI-U, published by the Bureau of Labor Statistics, is released monthly. It is used as a cost-of-living benchmark to adjust Social Security payments and other payment schedules, pay raises in multi-year union contracts, alimony, child support, and tax brackets. Inflation is measured by the consumer price index, which is also known as the *cost-of-living index.* (*Barron's Finance & Investment Handbook.*)

Gross Domestic Product (GDP). The GDP is the total market value of goods and services produced in the United States. The growth of the U.S. economy is measured by the change in the inflation-adjusted GDP, or the *real GDP.* (*Barron's Finance & Investment Handbook.*)

Index of Leading Economic Indicators. This index, published by the Conference Board, is a composite of ten economic indicators adjusted for inflation. The components of the index are:

1. Average work week of manufacturing production workers
2. Average weekly initial claims for unemployment insurance
3. New orders for consumer goods and materials
4. Vendor performance (companies receiving slower deliveries from suppliers)
5. New orders for nondefense capital goods
6. New building permits
7. Index of S&P 500 common stock prices
8. Money supply as measured by M-2
9. Index of consumer expectations
10. Interest rate spread, 10-year U.S. Treasury bond rate less federal funds rate

The index is designed to forecast economic strength and therefore is an important indicator for economists, investors, and business people.

Producer Price Index (PPI). This index measures average changes in selling prices received by domestic producers for their output. The PPI may be a leading indicator to the CPI. The PPI was formerly called the *wholesale price index.*

Unemployment Rate. The unemployment rate is the percentage of the civilian labor force actively looking for work but unable to find jobs. The unemployment rate is affected by the number of people entering the workforce as well as by the number of unemployed people. A rising unemployment rate may be seen by analysts and the Federal Reserve Board as a sign of a weakening economy, which might call for an easing of monetary policy (lowering interest rates) by the Fed. On the other hand, a drop in the unemployment rate may show that the economy is growing, which may indicate higher inflation, which may cause the Fed to tighten monetary policy (raising interest rates). (*Barron's Finance & Investment Handbook.*)

CHAPTER 8

Getting Mutual Fund Research Information

The mutual fund industry is not lacking research information about types of funds, investment objective categories, rankings, risks, portfolio holdings, performance, and other pertinent financial data. Some of the firms which provide information to the public include financial services firms, mutual fund management companies, research firms, and publishers of periodicals.

Financial Services Firms

Brokerage firms, banks with brokerage operations, and financial planning firms can provide you with prospectuses, research, historical market information, investing guides, and other pertinent information about numerous mutual funds and fund families. In addition, NYSE and NASD registered investment professionals employed by the firms are available to discuss with you the risks, potential returns, investment characteristics, underlying securities, and the historical performance of the mutual funds that are suitable for you.

In addition, the investment professionals are trained and educated in the area of asset allocation and the process of selecting the appropriate mutual funds for you based on your Investment Policy Statement. They are willing and able to assist you in formulating your Investment Policy Statement, including your risk tolerance, investment objectives, and financial condition.

The investment professionals have the latest technologies to create computer reports showing your current asset allocation, revised allocation, if a recommendation is necessary, and projections for college planning, retirement planning, and financial planning. Many of these services are provided to you without a cost or obligation. Financial services firms may subscribe to much of the research information from other sources described below, which they make available to you.

Mutual Fund Management Companies

Mutual fund management companies can provide you with prospectuses, research, historical market information, investing guides, and other pertinent information about their respective mutual funds. Mutual fund companies have computer reports that can show recommended asset allocation and projections for college planning, retirement planning, and financial planning.

Trade Organizations

Two major trade organizations that supply the mutual fund industry with current data from surveys, research studies, and legislation are Investment Company Institute and DALBAR, Inc.

Investment Company Institute

The Investment Company Institute is the national association of the United States investment company industry. Its membership, representing 95 percent of total industry assets, includes open-end investment companies (mutual funds), closed-end investment companies, and sponsors of unit investment trusts. The mutual fund members had assets of $3.6 trillion and had over 59 million individual shareholders in mid-1997.

DALBAR, Inc.

DALBAR, Inc. is a full-service information resource firm for the mutual fund industry. Since 1986, DALBAR has published a series of periodicals, industry surveys, and research studies regarding mutual fund management companies' services and customers' satisfaction. (Source: DALBAR, Inc., Boston, Mass.)

Mutual Fund Research Companies

Several research companies provide information to the public and the mutual fund industry. Some of the well-known companies are: (1) CDA/Wiesenberger; (2) Chase Global Data and Research; (3) Ibbotson Associates; (4) IBC Financial Data, Inc.; (5) Lipper Analytical Services, Inc.; (6) Moody's Investors Service, Inc.; (7) Morningstar, Inc.; (8) Standard & Poor's; and (9) Value Line Publishing, Inc.

CDA/Wiesenberger

CDA/Wiesenberger, a leader in mutual fund information, publishes the *CDA/Wiesenberger Mutual Funds Update* to provide investors with mutual funds data and information. The publication lists 24 investment objective categories under three broad sections. (Source: CDA/Wiesenberger.)

Chase Global Data and Research

Chase Data and Research has provided individuals and professionals a broad array of investment performance on over 360 major investments worldwide since 1960. The company publishes annually the *Chase Investment Performance Digest* and the *Investor's Guide to Investment Performance,* as well as *Investment View*® software. It covers more than 10,000 mutual funds and 360 indices, plus goal planner calculators and college and retirement planners. (Source: Chase Global Data & Research, 73 Junction Square, Concord, MA 01742.)

Ibbotson Associates

Ibbotson Associates is an investment software, consulting, and data products firm that focuses on providing historical asset performance, investment principles, asset allocation, and mutual fund analysis. (Source: Ibbotson Associates.)

IBC Financial Data, Inc.

IBC Financial Data, Inc. publishes *IBC's Money Fund Report,* which gives a full listing of money market funds, and averages information on performance trends, legislative changes, portfolio strategies, and cash management strategies for the universe of money market funds. (Source: IBC Financial Data, Inc.; http://www.ibcdata.com.)

Lipper Analytical Services, Inc.

Lipper Analytical Services is a leader for mutual fund information, performance returns and comparisons, and mutual fund indexes. Lipper classifies mutual funds by investment objective under 125 overall categories, including 34 equity categories and 91 fixed-income categories.

Moody's Investors Service, Inc.

Moody's, a leading provider of independent credit ratings, research, and financial information, publishes *Moody's Money Market and Bond Fund Ratings.* (Source: Moody's Investors Service, Inc.)

Morningstar, Inc.

Morningstar, Inc. is a leader in researching and recommending mutual funds. Morningstar, Inc. publishes *Morningstar Mutual Funds* and *Morningstar No-Load Funds,* which contain comprehensive and detailed reports about mutual funds.

Revised fund categories. In November 1996, Morningstar revised its mutual fund categories from the traditionally industry-accepted categories. The traditional method is categorizing mutual funds by investment objective, such as aggressive growth, growth, growth and income, and income. Morningstar now categorizes mutual funds based on the actual stocks and bonds in the fund's portfolios. The revised categories are designed to help the reader select funds with the best risk-adjusted returns within their peer groups.

Because the name of the fund and even the stated investment objective doesn't always match the underlying securities, the investor has a difficult time judging which securities are being held by the fund. Without that information, investors may not be able to adequately and efficiently allocate their assets according to their selected percentages for various types of securities. You may purchase two different funds, based on the name, that seem to have different types of securities, but which may be identical. Knowing the underlying securities is important because the price of the mutual fund's share is derived from the performance of the underlying securities, affecting your investment dollar.

Equity style. Morningstar divides equity style between domestic and international.

Domestic equity. Morningstar displays in a nine-box matrix form both the fund's investment approach and the size of the companies in which it invests. Horizontally, three investment styles are displayed:

1. Value-oriented
2. Growth-oriented
3. A blend of value and growth

Vertically, three size categories are displayed:

1. Large-cap
2. Mid-cap
3. Small-cap

Therefore, the combination of investment approach and size categories offers a broad view of a fund's holdings and risk. Within Morningstar's equity style box grid, nine possible combinations exist, ranging from large-cap value for the safest funds to small-cap growth for the riskiest.

FIGURE 8.1   Morningstar Equity Styles by Categories

Style	Range of Relative PE and PB
Value	Relative PE + relative PB less than 1.75
Blend	Relative PE + relative PB between 1.75 and 2.25
Growth	Relative PE + relative PB greater than 2.25

Market-capitalizations are categorized as follows: small-cap = less than $1 billion, mid-cap = between $1 billion and $5 billion, and large-cap = greater than $5 billion.

Equity styles are categorized by value, blend, and growth based on the fund's portfolio's average price-earnings (PE) ratios and price-book (PB) ratios relative to those of the S&P 500 Index over the past three years. Refer to Chapter 7 for an explanation of the S&P 500 Index. Figure 8.1 shows equity style categories for value, blend, and growth.

International equity. International-equity style boxes are similar to the domestic-equity style boxes with a couple of differences. Due to accounting differences internationally in calculating earnings, price to cash flow is used to give a more consistent analysis. The sum of the relative price–cash flow ratio and the relative price-book ratio determines the category of the stock. For the value, blend, and growth determination, price–cash flow ratios and price-book ratios are measured relative to the MSCI EAFE Index. Refer to Chapter 7 for an explanation of the MSCI EAFE Index.

Fixed-income style. Morningstar uses the same fixed-income style for both domestic and international.

Domestic and international. Morningstar displays in a nine-box matrix form both the fund's interest rate sensitivity and the credit quality of the fund's portfolio. Horizontally, the three categories of interest rate sensitivity as determined by the fund's portfolio average maturity length are:

1. Short
2. Intermediate
3. Long

Vertically, three categories of the fund's portfolio average credit quality are:

1. High quality
2. Medium quality
3. Low quality

Therefore, the combination of investment average maturity and average credit quality offers a broad view of a fund's holdings and risk. Within Morningstar's fixed-income style box grid, nine possible combinations exist, ranging from short maturity–high quality for the safest funds to long maturity–low quality for the riskiest.

Funds that hold bonds with an average maturity of four years or less are categorized as short-term. Funds that hold bonds with an average maturity of from more than four to ten years are categorized as intermediate-term. Funds that hold bonds with an average maturity of more than ten years are categorized as long-term.

Funds that hold bonds with an average credit rating of AAA or AA are categorized as high quality. Funds that hold bonds with an average credit rating of A or BBB are categorized as medium quality. Funds that hold bonds with an average credit rating of BB or lower are categorized as low quality. Credit ratings of AAA, AA, A, BBB, and BB are provided by Standard & Poor's. (Source: Morningstar, Inc.)

Standard & Poor's

Standard & Poor's, a leading provider of independent credit ratings, research, and financial information, publishes *Standard & Poor's/ Lipper Mutual Fund Profiles* that reviews performance, portfolio composition, and other pertinent financial information. (Source: Standard & Poor's.)

Value Line Publishing, Inc.

Value Line Publishing, Inc., a leading investment research firm, offers *The Value Line Mutual Fund Survey* that contains three parts:

1. Performance & Index
2. Ratings & Reports
3. Value Line Mutual Fund Adviser

Value Line uses 31 stock and bond categories to classify mutual funds, with another 55 subpeer groups to allow for meaningful comparisons of funds that follow more specialized or style-specific approaches. A unique manager rating shows the risk-adjusted performance of individual managers, and advanced style attribution analysis is used to help investors implement and maintain an asset allocation strategy.

Performance & Index. Part 1 summarizes the prices, returns, yields, and rankings for risks and performance.

Ratings & Reports. Part 2 provides a detailed report about individual funds. Information includes recent developments and strategies, management style, financial data, past performance, portfolio holdings, and other pertinent information.

Value Line Mutual Fund Adviser. Part 3 is a newsletter that discusses individual topics related to mutual fund investing. (Source: *Value Line Mutual Fund Survey,* New York, NY.)

Periodicals

Many periodicals provide information about mutual funds. Some of the more well-known publications are:

- *The Wall Street Journal*
- *Barron's*
- *Investor's Business Daily*
- *The New York Times*
- *USA Today*
- *Forbes*
- *Business Week*
- *Kiplinger's Personal Finance Magazine*
- *Fortune*
- *Money*
- *Worth*
- *Mutual Funds*
- *Your Money*
- *Financial World*
- *Time*
- *U.S. News & World Report*

CHAPTER 9

Profiling Mutual Funds

As mentioned throughout this book, the important consideration when investing in mutual funds is to identify your investment objective, the fund's investment objective, the fund's underlying securities, and risk considerations. Your investment objective is unique to you. Therefore, you need to invest in mutual funds that are suitable for your investment objective(s) and risk tolerance. Once you have purchased a fund's shares, you need to monitor if the fund's performance is meeting your expectations. Comparing your fund's total return to an absolute number, a risk-free return, market indexes, or mutual fund indexes are methods for you to determine your fund's relative performance.

Following are several types of mutual funds with their risk considerations, comparable market indexes, and comparable mutual fund indexes. In most cases, several indexes are listed. You should select the most appropriate index depending on the particular type of fund you own.

Money Market Mutual Funds with Their Risks and Comparable Indexes

Taxable Money Market Fund

- *Risk.* The fund is not insured or guaranteed by the U.S. Government or the FDIC, and therefore no assurance can be made that the fund will maintain a stable net asset value of $1. The yield will fluctuate based on the changing interest rates in the marketplace.
- *Market index comparison.* The 90-day certificates of deposit rate or the 90-day U.S. Treasury bill rate.
- *Mutual fund index comparison.* Lipper Money Market Funds Index.

Tax-Exempt Money Market Fund

- *Risk.* The fund is not insured or guaranteed by the U.S. Government or the FDIC and, therefore, no assurance can be made that the fund will maintain a stable net asset value of $1. The yield will fluctuate based on the changing interest rates in the marketplace.
- *Market index comparison.* The after-tax return (using your tax bracket) of the 90-day certificates of deposit rate or the 90-day U.S. Treasury bill rate.
- *Mutual fund index comparison.* Lipper Tax-exempt Money Market Funds Index.

Taxable Bond Mutual Funds with Their Risks and Comparable Indexes

Government Securities Fund

- *Risk.* The value or yield of the shares of the fund is not guaranteed by the government or any agency thereof. Likewise, the value or the yield of the government securities invested in by the fund is not guaranteed by the U.S. Government or any agency thereof. The prices of bonds are, generally, inversely affected by changes in interest rates and, therefore, are subject to the risk of market price fluctuations.

- *Market index comparison.* Lehman Brothers Government Bond Index (Intermediate-Term Index or Long-Term Index, depending on the portfolio's average length of maturity).
- *Mutual fund index comparison.* Lipper General U.S. Government Funds Index and CDA/Wiesenberger Income Index.

Long-Term Corporate Bond Fund

- *Risk.* The prices of corporate bonds are, generally, inversely affected by changes in interest rates and, therefore, are subject to the risk of market price fluctuations. The value of bonds also may be affected by changes in the credit rating or financial condition of the issuing entities.
- *Market index comparison.* Lehman Brothers Long Corporate Bond Index, Salomon Brothers High-Grade Corporate Index, Dow Jones 20 Bond Average, and Merrill Lynch Corporate Master Index.
- *Mutual fund index comparison.* Lipper Corporate Debt Funds Index and CDA/Wiesenberger Income Index.

Intermediate Corporate Bond Fund

- *Risk.* The prices of corporate bonds are, generally, inversely affected by changes in interest rates and, therefore, are subject to the risk of market price fluctuations. The value of bonds also may be affected by changes in the credit rating or financial condition of the issuing entities.
- *Market index comparison.* Lehman Brothers Intermediate Corporate Bond Index and Merrill Lynch Corporate 1–9.99 Year Index.
- *Mutual fund index comparison.* Lipper Intermediate Investment Grade Debt Funds Index and CDA/Wiesenberger Income Index.

High Yield Corporate Bond Fund

- *Risk.* Compared with higher rated, lower yielding notes and bonds, portfolio securities of the fund may be subject to greater risk of loss of income and principal and greater risk of increases and decreases in net asset value due to market fluctuations. The prices of corporate bonds are, generally, inversely affected by changes in interest rates and, therefore, are subject to the risk of market price fluctuations. The value of bonds also may be affected by changes in the credit rating or financial condition of the issuing entities. Lower quality (rated Ba or lower by Moody's or BB or lower by Standard & Poor's) bonds, sometimes called junk bonds, have a greater risk of default or bankruptcy by the issuer.
- *Market index comparison.* Lehman Brothers High Yield Bond Index and Credit Suisse First Boston High Yield Index.
- *Mutual fund index comparison.* Lipper High Current Yield Funds Index.

International Government Bond Fund

- *Risk.* The prices of bonds are, generally, inversely affected by changes in interest rates and, therefore, are subject to the risk of market price fluctuations. The value of bonds also may be affected by changes in the credit rating or financial condition of the issuing entities. Foreign securities investments may be affected by changes in currency rates or exchange control regulations, changes in government administration or economic or monetary policy (in the United States and abroad), or changed circumstances in dealings between nations. Fluctuations in the relative rates of exchange between the currencies of different nations will affect the value of the fund's investments denominated in foreign currency. Investing internationally poses more political and economic uncertainty than investing in the United States.
- *Market index comparison.* Salomon Brothers Non–U.S. Dollar World Government Bond Index.[SM]

- *Mutual fund index comparison.* Lipper General World Income Funds Index.

Global Government Bond Fund

- *Risk.* The prices of bonds are, generally, inversely affected by changes in interest rates and, therefore, are subject to the risk of market price fluctuations. The value of bonds also may be affected by changes in the credit rating or financial condition of the issuing entities. Foreign securities investments may be affected by changes in currency rates or exchange control regulations, changes in government administration or economic or monetary policy (in the United States and abroad), or changed circumstances in dealings between nations. Fluctuations in the relative rates of exchange between the currencies of different nations will affect the value of the fund's investments denominated in foreign currency. Investing internationally poses more political and economic uncertainty than investing in the United States.
- *Market index comparison.* Salomon Brothers World Government Bond Index.[SM]
- *Mutual fund index comparison.* Lipper General World Income Funds Index.

Tax-Exempt Bond Mutual Funds with Their Risks and Comparable Indexes

Tax-Exempt Bond Fund–National

- *Risk.* The prices of municipal bonds are, generally, inversely affected by changes in interest rates and, therefore, are subject to the risk of market price fluctuations. The value of bonds also may be affected by changes in the credit rating or financial condition of the issuing entities.
- *Market index comparison.* The Bond Buyer Index, The 20-Bond Buyer Index, The 11-Bond Buyer Index, and Lehman Brothers Municipal Bond Index.
- *Mutual fund index comparison.* Lipper General Municipal Debt Funds Index.

Tax-Exempt Bond Fund—Single State

- *Risk.* The prices of municipal bonds are, generally, inversely affected by changes in interest rates and, therefore, are subject to the risk of market price fluctuations. The value of bonds also may be affected by changes in the credit rating or financial condition of the issuing entities.
- *Market index comparison.* The Bond Buyer Index, The 20-Bond Buyer Index, The 11-Bond Buyer Index, and Lehman Brothers Municipal Bond Index.
- *Mutual fund index comparison.* Lipper (State) Municipal Debt Funds Index.

Stock Mutual Funds with Their Risks and Comparable Indexes

Aggressive Growth Fund

- *Risk.* Investing in lesser known, smaller capitalization companies may involve greater risk of volatility in the fund's net asset value than is customarily associated with larger, more established companies. The net asset value of the fund's shares fluctuates with changes in the market value of its portfolio's underlying securities. The fund's primary holdings are common stocks, which may be extremely volatile over the short term.
- *Market index comparison.* S&P 600 SmallCap Index, Nasdaq Small-Cap Index, Russell 2000 Index, and Russell 2000 Growth Index.
- *Mutual fund index comparison.* Lipper Capital Appreciation Index, Lipper Small Company Growth Funds Index, and CDA/Wiesenberger Growth Index.

Small-Cap Growth Fund

- *Risk.* Investing in lesser known, smaller capitalization companies may involve greater risk of volatility in the fund's net asset value than is customarily associated with larger, more established companies. The net asset value of the fund's shares fluctuates with changes in the market value of its portfolio underlying securities. The fund's primary holdings are common stocks, which may be extremely volatile over the short term.

- *Market index comparison.* S&P 600 SmallCap Index, Nasdaq Small-Cap Index, Russell 2000 Index, and Russell 2000 Growth Index.
- *Mutual fund index comparison.* Lipper Capital Appreciation Index, Lipper Small Company Growth Funds Index, and CDA/Wiesenberger Growth Index.

Mid-Cap Fund

- *Risk.* The net asset value of the fund's shares fluctuates with changes in the market value of its portfolio's underlying securities. The fund's primary holdings are common stocks, which may be volatile over the short term.
- *Market index comparison.* S&P 400 MidCap Index, S&P Mid-Cap 400/BARRA Growth Index, S&P MidCap 400/BARRA Value Index, Russell Midcap Index, and the Nasdaq Composite.
- *Mutual fund index comparison.* Lipper MidCap Funds Index and CDA/Wiesenberger Growth Index.

Large-Cap Fund

- *Risk.* The net asset value of the fund's shares fluctuates with changes in the market value of its portfolio's underlying securities. The fund's primary holdings are common stocks, which may be volatile over the short term. Dividends payable by the fund will vary in relation to the amount of dividends earned by the portfolio's securities.
- *Market index comparison.* Dow Jones Industrial Average, S&P 400 Industrial Index, and Russell Top 200 Index.
- *Mutual fund index comparison.* Lipper Growth and Income Funds Index and CDA/Wiesenberger Growth/Income Index.

Growth Fund

- *Risk*. The net asset value of the fund's shares fluctuates with changes in the market value of its portfolio's underlying securities. The fund's primary holdings are common stocks, which may be volatile over the short term.
- *Market index comparison*. S&P 500 Index, S&P 400 Industrial Index, S&P 500/BARRA Growth Index, Russell 1000 Index, and Russell 1000 Growth Index.
- *Mutual fund index comparison*. Lipper Growth Funds Index and CDA/Wiesenberger Growth Index.

Value Fund

- *Risk*. The net asset value of the fund's shares fluctuates with changes in the market value of its portfolio's underlying securities. The fund's primary holdings are common stocks, which may be volatile over the short term. Dividends payable by the fund will vary in relation to the amount of dividends earned by the portfolio securities.
- *Market index comparison*. S&P 500 Index, S&P 400 Industrial Index, S&P 500/BARRA Value Index, Russell 1000 Index, and Russell 1000 Value Index.
- *Mutual fund index comparison*. Lipper Growth and Income Funds Index and CDA/Wiesenberger Growth/Income Index.

Growth and Income Fund

- *Risk*. The net asset value of the fund's shares fluctuates with changes in the market value of its portfolio's underlying securities. The fund's primary holdings are common stocks, which may be volatile over the short term. Dividends payable by the fund will vary in relation to the amount of dividends earned by the portfolio's securities.
- *Market index comparison*. Dow Jones Industrial Average, S&P 400 Industrial Index, and Russell Top 200 Index.
- *Mutual fund index comparison*. Lipper Growth and Income Funds Index and CDA/Wiesenberger Growth/Income Index.

Equity Income Fund

- *Risk.* The net asset value of the fund's shares fluctuates with changes in the market value of its portfolio's underlying securities. The fund's primary holdings are common stocks, which may be volatile over the short term. Dividends payable by the fund will vary in relation to the amount of dividends earned by the portfolio's securities.
- *Market index comparison.* Dow Jones Utilities Average, S&P 40 Utilities Index, and Russell Top 200.
- *Mutual fund index comparison.* Lipper Equity Income Funds Index and CDA/Wiesenberger Growth/Income Index.

Index Fund

- *Risk.* The net asset value of the fund's shares fluctuates with changes in the market value of its portfolio's underlying securities. The fund may engage in transactions involving stock index futures contracts. The fund's primary holdings are common stocks, which may be volatile over the short term.
- *Market index comparison.* S&P 500 Index, S&P 400 MidCap Index, S&P 600 SmallCap Index, Dow Jones Industrial Average, Russell 3000 Index, Russell 2000 Index, and the Wilshire 5000 Equity Index.
- *Mutual fund index comparison.* Lipper S&P 500 Index Objective Funds Index and CDA/Wiesenberger Growth Index.

Sector Fund–Technology

- *Risk.* Unlike more widely diversified mutual funds, this fund is subject to industry risk such as the possibility that a particular group of related stocks will decline in price. The technology and computer industry generally is subject to rapid changes that could have a material effect on the demand for products and services offered by technology and computer companies, and therefore, could affect the performance of the fund. The net asset value of the fund's shares fluctuates with changes in the market value of its portfolio's underlying securities. The fund's primary holdings are common stocks, which may be extremely volatile over the short term.

- *Market index comparison.* S&P 500/BARRA Growth Index, S&P 400 Industrial Index, Russell 3000 Growth Index, and Nasdaq 100 Index.
- *Mutual fund index comparison.* Lipper Science and Technology Funds Index and CDA/Wiesenberger Growth Index.

Utility Fund

- *Risk.* The public utilities industry has certain characteristics and risks, and developments within the industry that affect the fund's portfolio. The net asset value of the fund's shares fluctuates with changes in the market value of its portfolio's underlying securities. The fund's primary holdings are common stocks, which may be volatile over the short term.
- *Market index comparison.* Dow Jones Utilities Average and S&P 40 Utilities Index.
- *Mutual fund index comparison.* Lipper Utility Funds Index and CDA/Wiesenberger Growth/Income Index.

International Small-Cap Fund

- *Risk.* Investing in lesser known, smaller capitalization companies may involve greater risk of volatility in the fund's net asset value than is customarily associated with larger, more established companies. Typically, there is less publicly available information concerning foreign and smaller companies than for domestic and larger, more established companies. Also, because smaller companies normally have fewer shares outstanding than larger companies and trade less frequently, it may be more difficult for the fund to buy and sell significant amounts of such shares without an unfavorable impact on prevailing market prices.

    Foreign securities investments may be affected by changes in currency rates or exchange control regulations, changes in government administration or economic or monetary policy (in the United States and abroad), or changed circumstances in dealings between nations. Fluctuations in the relative rates of exchange between the currencies of different nations will affect the value of the fund's investments denominated in foreign currency. Investing internationally poses more political and economic uncertainty than investing in the United States. The fund's primary holdings are common stocks, which may be extremely volatile over the short term.

- *Market index comparison.* Morgan Stanley Capital International Europe, Australasia, Far East Index (MSCI EAFE).
- *Mutual fund index comparison.* Lipper International Funds Index.

International Growth Fund

- *Risk.* Typically, there is less publicly available information concerning foreign and smaller companies than for domestic and larger, more established companies. Also, because smaller companies normally have fewer shares outstanding than larger companies and trade less frequently, it may be more difficult for the fund to buy and sell significant amounts of such shares without an unfavorable impact on prevailing market prices.

  Foreign securities investments may be affected by changes in currency rates or exchange control regulations, changes in government administration or economic or monetary policy (in the United States and abroad), or changed circumstances in dealings between nations. Fluctuations in the relative rates of exchange between the currencies of different nations will affect the value of the fund's investments denominated in foreign currency. Investing internationally poses more political and economic uncertainty than investing in the United States. The fund's primary holdings are common stocks, which may be extremely volatile over the short term.

- *Market index comparison.* Morgan Stanley Capital International Europe, Australasia, Far East Index (MSCI EAFE), All Ordinaires Index, ASX All Ordinaires Price Index, DAX Index, FT-SE 100 Index, Hang Seng Index, Nikkei 225 Index, Paris CAC-40 Index, SES All-Singapore Index, or Toronto 300 Composite Index, depending on the portfolio's composition.
- *Mutual fund index comparison.* Lipper International Funds Index.

Single-Country Fund

- *Risk.* Unlike more widely diversified mutual funds, the single-country fund is subject to the sole country's economic, political, and market risks. Typically, there is less publicly available information concerning foreign companies than for domestic established companies. Foreign securities investments may be affected by changes in currency rates or exchange control regulations, changes in government administration or economic or monetary policy (in the United States and abroad), or changed circumstances in dealings between nations. Fluctuations in the relative rates of exchange between the currencies of different nations will affect the value of the fund's investments denominated in foreign currency. Investing internationally poses more political and economic uncertainty than investing in the United States. The fund's primary holdings are common stocks, which may be extremely volatile over the short term.
- *Market index comparison.* All Ordinaires Index, ASX All Ordinaires Price Index, DAX Index, FT-SE 100 Index, Hang Seng Index, Nikkei 225 Index, Paris CAC-40 Index, SES All-Singapore Index, or Toronto 300 Composite Index, depending on the country.
- *Mutual fund index comparison.* Lipper Pacific Region Funds Index, Lipper European Funds Index, depending on the country.

Region Fund

- *Risk.* Foreign securities and markets in which the fund invests pose different and greater risks than those customarily associated with domestic securities and their markets. Typically, there is less publicly available information concerning foreign companies than for domestic companies. Foreign securities investments may be affected by changes in currency rates or exchange control regulations, changes in government administration or economic or monetary policy (in the United States and abroad), or changed circumstances in dealings between nations. Fluctuations in the relative rates of exchange between the currencies of different nations will affect the value of the fund's investments denominated in foreign currency. Investing internationally poses more political and economic uncertainty than investing in the United States. The fund's primary holdings are common stocks, which may be extremely volatile over the short term.

- *Market index comparison.* All Ordinaires Index, ASX All Ordinaires Price Index, DAX Index, FT-SE 100 Index, Hang Seng Index, Nikkei 225 Index, Paris CAC-40 Index, SES All-Singapore Index, or Toronto 300 Composite Index, depending on the region.
- *Mutual fund index comparison.* Lipper Pacific Region Funds Index or Lipper European Funds Index, depending on the region.

Mixed Mutual Funds with Their Risks and Comparable Indexes

Asset Allocation Fund

- *Risk.* The net asset value of the fund's shares fluctuates with changes in the market value of its portfolio's underlying securities. The fund's holdings are common stocks, which may be volatile over the short term, and bonds, which values are generally inversely affected by changes in interest rates and, therefore, are subject to the risk of market price fluctuations. The value of bonds also may be affected by changes in the credit rating or financial condition of the issuing entities.
- *Market index comparison.* A percent mix of 60 percent S&P 500 Index, 30 percent Lehman Brothers Intermediate Government/Corporate Index, and 10 percent U.S. Treasury bill (90 days), or 60 percent Russell 1000 Index, 30 percent Lehman Brothers Intermediate Government/Corporate Index, and 10 percent U.S. Treasury bill (90 days), or 60 percent Dow Jones Industrial Average, 30 percent Lehman Brothers Intermediate Government/Corporate Index, and 10 percent U.S. Treasury bill (90 days). The percentages may vary depending on the allocation of the portfolio's assets.
- *Mutual fund index comparison.* Lipper Flexible Portfolio Funds Index.

Balanced Growth Fund

- *Risk.* The net asset value of the fund's shares fluctuates with changes in the market value of its portfolio's underlying securities. The fund's holdings are common stocks, which may be extremely volatile over the short term, and bonds, which values are generally inversely affected by changes in interest rates and, therefore, are subject to the risk of market price fluctuations. The value of bonds also may be affected by changes in the credit rating or financial condition of the issuing entities.
- *Market index comparison.* A percent mix of 60 percent S&P 500 Index, 30 percent Lehman Brothers Intermediate Government/Corporate Index, and 10 percent U.S. Treasury bill (90 days), or 60 percent Russell 1000 Index, 30 percent Lehman Brothers Intermediate Government/Corporate Index, and 10 percent U.S. Treasury bill (90 days), or 60 percent Dow Jones Industrial Average, 30 percent Lehman Brothers Intermediate Government/Corporate Index, and 10 percent U.S. Treasury bill (90 days). The percentages may vary depending on the general allocation of the portfolio's assets.
- *Mutual fund index comparison.* Lipper Flexible Portfolio Funds Index.

Balanced Income Fund

- *Risk.* The net asset value of the fund's shares fluctuates with changes in the market value of its portfolio's underlying securities. The fund's holdings are common stocks, which may be volatile over the short term, and bonds, which values are generally inversely affected by changes in interest rates and, therefore, are subject to the risk of market price fluctuations. The value of bonds also may be affected by changes in the credit rating or financial condition of the issuing entities.
- *Market index comparison.* A percent mix of 30 percent S&P 500 Index, 60 percent Lehman Brothers Intermediate Government/Corporate Index, and 10 percent U.S. Treasury bill (90 days), or 30 percent Russell 1000 Index, 60 percent Lehman Brothers Intermediate Government/Corporate Index, and 10

percent U.S. Treasury bill (90 days), or 30 percent Dow Jones Industrial Average, 60 percent Lehman Brothers Intermediate Government/Corporate Index, and 10 percent U.S. Treasury bill (90 days). The percentages may vary depending on the allocation of the portfolio's assets.

- *Mutual fund index comparison.* Lipper Flexible Portfolio Funds Index.

CHAPTER 10

Writing Your Investment Policy Statement

Portfolio management is the process of structuring and adjusting your investment assets to create a profitable portfolio appropriate for your age, financial needs, and investment goals. Monitoring the economy, marketplaces, and your mutual funds is an ongoing process, year in and year out. Your investment objectives and type of portfolio dictate how often and detailed the monitoring and adjusting need to be.

Some investors purchase securities for long-term capital appreciation or for a steady income. Others trade securities for short-term profits. The quality of the investments may influence how much time is required to monitor the securities; the riskier the investment, the closer it must be watched. The investment mix of different types of mutual funds and asset categories provides you the opportunity to meet your investment objective and earn a desirable rate of return on your investment.

Structuring and managing your own portfolio is a long-term process. It is not just deciding that you want to invest and buy different securities because they sound good and appear to be potentially profit-able. Structuring your portfolio is like building a house. When you build a house, the basic procedure is to select the architect and builder, design the house, choose the materials, and devise a time schedule for comple-tion. Similarly, when you build an investment portfolio, you should set your goals, design the portfolio, choose the securities, and create a time schedule to make the investments. Your house needs to fit your lifestyle and meet your personal needs; your portfolio needs to fit your invest-ment objectives and meet your financial needs.

You should prepare your personal *investment policy statement* be-fore you begin investing. An investment policy statement provides a framework for making investment decisions that are appropriate for you in relation to your investment objectives, risk tolerance, financial condi-tion, and other factors. If you are investing currently, you should prepare one as well. The steps to create a viable investment policy statement are:

- Prepare your investor's profile.
- Understand your risks and returns.
- Allocate your assets.
- Select your mutual funds.
- Measure your risks and returns.
- Monitor your mutual funds' performances.
- Review your portfolio and investment policy statement.

Examine your investment policy statement in detail—on your own or with your investment professional (see Chapter 2).

Preparing Your Investor's Profile

Preparing your investor's profile is both subjective and objective. Take enough time to do the job well—it's your future you're planning. To establish your profile, you need to examine your personal investment goals and objectives, risk tolerances, return expectations, financial assets, income, age, health, family obligations, and investment experi-ence. Discussing your profile with an investment professional helps you clarify why and how you want to invest. Knowing and understanding the specific aspects of your profile permits you to make your investment decisions easier, better, and more informed. Writing down your profile allows you to review it periodically. Providing a copy to your investment professional assists him or her in making appropriate investment recommendations to you. Your investment professional should have a form or questionnaire to assist you in formulating your investor's profile.

Financial Condition

Creating a *personal financial statement,* also known as a *balance sheet*, enables you to look at your entire current financial picture, including your assets, liabilities, and net worth. First, list both your assets (things you own) and liabilities (debts) separately. Then determine your *net worth* by subtracting liabilities from assets.

Assets are those financial items that you own or that are owed to you. Assets include, but are not limited to, current worth of automobiles; cash value of insurance policies; savings accounts; stocks and bonds; CDs; real estate; and personal items, such as clothing, furniture, and jewelry. Another type of asset you may have is a receivable. A *receivable* is anything that a person expects to receive from another individual, such as a "loan payable to you." Add up all your assets.

When most people own something, they have either paid for it or have borrowed money to buy it. The portion that was borrowed to pay for the asset is a *liability.* Therefore, when you buy an asset such as a house, you borrow money in the form of a mortgage, which is a liability. Other liabilities include credit card balances, car loans, any money borrowed against the cash value of a life insurance policy, and items that are required to be paid to a corporation, person, or government, such as interest and taxes. Add up all your liabilities.

To figure your net worth, subtract your total liabilities from your total assets. If your net worth is positive, you are considered solvent and in "good" financial condition. If your net worth is negative, you are considered insolvent and in "bad" financial condition.

Your assets and liabilities will fluctuate over time, but what is important is that your net worth increases. Therefore, you need to calculate your net worth periodically to make sure you are successfully improving your financial condition. Knowing your net worth is an excellent way to begin building your financial security. Updating your personal financial statement annually or whenever a major financial change has taken place will help you know your financial condition. There are many good computer programs to help you keep track of your personal finances—including investments and taxes. Before choosing one, be sure it contains a financial statement or net worth module. (See also Your Investor's Guide at the end of this chapter that includes a financial statement.)

Investment Goals

Life is a series of goals. Achieving financial security is a vital one. Most people have many diverse goals when investing their assets. Your job is to identify and prioritize these goals and form them into a comprehensive investment goal. Writing your goals on a piece of paper helps define and prioritize them. Reviewing your investment goals annually helps you stay on track toward meeting them.

Your first step is to outline and then organize your investment goals. The best way of doing this is to make a list describing exactly where you want to be financially in one, three, five, and ten years, or longer. The list should contain not only the dollar amount to be accumulated, but also the purpose of the assets. Try to be as exact as possible with the numbers, such as $10 thousand, $50 thousand, $100 thousand, etc. You should also be as specific as possible in stating the goal of the investments, for example, build or buy a house, create a college fund, purchase a boat or car, or establish a retirement fund.

Your next step is to calculate how much money you have to invest now and how much you will be able to invest in the future. Try to pay yourself each payday by investing 10 percent of your income. This ensures that you budget a predetermined amount to be invested regularly rather than waiting for some "extra" money to be available.

Knowing Your Investment Objectives

When you buy real estate, the REALTOR® always emphasizes, "location, location, location." *When you invest in securities, the emphasis is "investment objective, investment objective, investment objective."* Once you know your objective(s), based on your investment goals, you are ready to make the appropriate investment selection (with or without the help of an investment professional).

"I want to make money!" This is the most common "investment objective" investment professionals hear from their clients. It is absolutely true that people want to make money, however, the statement is not so

simple: Do you want to receive money now? Do you want to receive money later? Do you want a combination of both? Are you willing to take a higher risk to make your money grow quickly, or are you willing to let it grow more slowly, yet steadily? What are the tax considerations when you make more money? Are you willing to lose some of your money while trying to make more? All of these questions have to be asked and answered to best achieve the *"I want to make money!"* objective.

Primary investment objectives. Based on your age, emotional makeup, current and long-term goals, employment status, financial condition, health, income, and lifestyle, your investment objectives will change over time. Three primary investment objectives are:

1. Preservation of principal
2. Income from the investment
3. Increase in value of invested capital (capital appreciation)

Capital appreciation is also known as *growth*. Usually, investors want some income from their investments while they wait for the investment to increase in value. And even though investors may want an income-producing investment, they may still want the income reinvested in the same security. They like to see their investment increase in value (outpace inflation) by the accumulation of the income earned. Therefore, one of the primary questions you must answer is, "Do you want income and/or growth investments?"

Specific investment objectives. Every investor has several investment objectives. Each mutual fund has different characteristics that may meet one or two investment objectives. Let's look at the most common investment objectives:

- *Preservation of capital.* One aim of a well-balanced portfolio is to ensure that the initial investment does not decline in value. If you are not able to replace the capital, the need for a secure investment is even more important to you. Adding "safe" financial investments to your portfolio, such as those in which the principal and interest are insured or guaranteed, may be an important step in achieving this vital investment goal.

- *Safety of principal.* Safety of principal is a measure of the likelihood that the principal value of the investment will be paid to you at maturity, or when you need it.
- *Income.* Some of the investments for a portfolio may be chosen to provide a steady stream of income. This income can be used either to meet current expenses or for reinvestment purposes. Income can add significantly to your total return.
- *Safety of income.* Safety of income is a measure of the likelihood that anticipated income from an investment will continue to be paid in the amount and at the time expected.
- *Growth of income.* Growth of income means that the income you receive from an investment increases over time. Growth of income is important so you can keep up with inflation and at least maintain your purchasing power.
- *Growth or capital appreciation.* An investment's value may grow, or appreciate, because of changing market conditions or due to the success of a business operation. Over the long term, the return from capital appreciation can be an important factor when you try to accumulate larger sums of money. Consider holding some growth-oriented investments in your portfolio to minimize inflation risk.

Types of Investors

Because each person is unique, you will have very definite, very individual, investment objectives. However, many people fall into common categories, such as the following:

Retired person. A retired person usually prefers investments that offer a good income with stability of principal. However, because people are living longer than ever before, retired people may need to still invest in growth mutual funds in order to maintain their accustomed lifestyle and keep up with inflation. Because each investor is different, the type of growth mutual fund must be appropriate to the investor's profile.

Middle-aged person. A middle-aged person may want a combination of income-oriented and growth-oriented investments to supplement his or her salary, as well as build assets for a second home, travel, or retirement.

Young person. A young person may want a growth-oriented investment in order to accumulate more assets for a first home, travel, or early retirement.

Child. Parents and grandparents may invest for a child's education and future benefit. An income-oriented investment or a growth-oriented investment may be used depending on the market outlook and risk aversion. The child's age is a major factor of how to invest the money. Typically, the younger the child, the more growth-oriented the investment may be. If the child is nearing the age where he or she may need the money for college, the mutual fund investment may be changed to a more conservative, stable investment.

High tax-bracket person. A high tax-bracket person may want tax-free or tax-deferred income investments. Additionally, this type of investor may want capital appreciation whereby no taxes are due until the investment is sold. The tax bracket often dictates the types of investments a person should purchase.

Fear and Greed

Many people experience two overriding emotions when investing: the fear of losing money and the greed for making more money. For instance, if you fear losing money, you may be reluctant to purchase higher risk investments even though they may offer higher returns. On the other hand, you may become greedy in trying to achieve additional profits and may buy unsuitable investments.

It is important for you to know and understand the various potential risks and rewards when investing because considering these two factors affects how and why you invest. The common way of knowing whether you are making money or losing money is to calculate a percent return. Numbers are always interesting to figure because they can be calculated in many different ways.

FIGURE 10.1   A Sample Allocation of Three Types of Money

Type of Money	Percent
Risk Money	5%
Investment Money	70
Serious Money	25

Level of Risk and Return

Because each investment comes with risk and return, it is best to determine how much risk you are willing to take and how much return you want. Some of your assets may be considered your serious money—money that you do not want to risk. Some of your assets may be your investment money—money on which you want to make a good return with reasonable risk. The rest of your assets may be your risk money—money on which you want to make a big return, so you may try a higher risk investment because you can tolerate losing some or all of it (see Figure 10.1).

Your percentages may differ from those in Figure 10.1 based on your age, financial condition, health, investment objectives, personal preference, and risk tolerance. Complete Your Investor's Guide with your own percentages for the three types of money.

Your Investor's Guide

Types of Money

Types of Money	Percent
Risk Money	_____ %
Investment Money	_____ %
Serious Money	_____ %

How Much Risk, How Much Return?

Three other important numbers you need to determine are:

1. The amount of risk you are willing to accept on your investment
2. The amount of total return you expect from your investment
3. The time horizon for each investment

These three factors will dictate what types of mutual funds you should purchase. Are you willing to lose 5 percent, 10 percent, 15 percent, 20 percent, or more while you wait to make a profit? Do you want a total return of 5 percent, 10 percent, 15 percent, or more? What percentage return is reasonable for you? When do you want to achieve a particular return? Do you need your money in six months, one year, five years, ten years, or longer?

Risk tolerance. Some people are completely adverse to any risk and others will assume any type of risk. Most people fall within these two extremes. When you invest in stock or bond mutual funds, you are assuming some degree of risk. The amount of risk is determined primarily by the type of underlying securities held in the fund. The general market performance for the underlying securities determines the volatility and performance for that mutual fund.

Purchasing 90-day U.S. Treasury bills is considered risk-free, even though the market price of the bills fluctuates until maturity date. In a "normal" interest rate environment, U.S. Treasury bills offer a safe but low return. Therefore, to achieve a better return than the risk-free rate of return, you must invest in an investment that offers more return, but at a greater risk. The amount of risk is directly related to your investor's profile and the time horizon to accomplish your investment goals.

Expected return. Expected return is always difficult to evaluate because most people want to make as much as they can. Reality is that achieving extremely high returns consistently is rare in any marketplace. Your expected return should be in light of the historical returns for the investment category and the returns currently being achieved.

Determining your expected return assists you in allocating your assets and selecting the appropriate mutual funds that may achieve your expected return. Selecting a return of 6 percent, 8 percent, 10 percent,

12 percent, 14 percent, or more may dictate which specific types of funds you should purchase. Even with the best-laid plans, you may achieve lower returns than expected—or higher!

The axiom "the greater the risk, the greater the *potential* return," usually holds true. Sometimes it is better to achieve a safer, moderate return than to aim for a higher return and lose capital.

Review with your investment professional the historical returns for stock mutual funds, bond mutual funds, and money market funds. Within each of the categories, numerous funds that hold different types of underlying securities offer various risks and returns.

Your time horizon. Besides risk and expected return, another major factor that determines the types of mutual funds to invest in is your time horizon (goal date) to achieve your investment goals. Your time horizon, along with your risk tolerance and expected returns, will dictate what types of mutual funds you should purchase. Certain types of mutual funds are suitable for you depending on their time horizon.

Liquidity—the ability to turn your assets into cash from an investment—is an important consideration in determining your time horizon and the appropriate type of mutual fund to purchase. Mutual funds are liquid (redeem into cash) every day that the New York Stock Exchange is open for business. The critical point is whether the time is right to sell (redeem) the shares of the mutual fund based on the level of the stock or bond market. If you need your money to purchase a home in one year, a stock mutual fund is probably not appropriate for you. If, however, you don't need your money until five years from now, a stock mutual fund could be appropriate for you.

Likewise, the investment outlook may be promising for the next six months, but because of sales charges, expenses, and fees in the mutual fund, it may not be as profitable to invest just for the six months. Mutual funds are generally considered long-term investments. The mutual fund's investment objective and volatility (risk) should be compatible with your time horizon for the money being invested.

Now that you have analyzed and reviewed your personal objectives, risk tolerance, and time horizon, it is time to look at fund families, types of funds, investment professionals, and fund cost structures.

Mutual Fund Family

Before you select individual mutual funds, the selection of one or two mutual fund families should be made. The mutual fund group is probably as important as the individual mutual funds because of the following seven reasons:

1. The number of different types of mutual funds in the family to select
2. The shareholder services that the management company provides
3. The investment professional with whom you discuss your investor's profile
4. The performance of the funds
5. The reputation of the management company
6. The cost structure of the funds
7. The ease of placing orders

Number of Different Types of Mutual Funds in the Family to Select

Two of the key components of portfolio management are asset allocation and diversification. Many mutual funds offer similar types of investment objectives with similar types of underlying securities. In Your Investor's Guide—Types of Money earlier in this chapter, you made asset allocation decisions. Asset allocation is a dominant factor in achieving significant returns. A well-balanced portfolio should have different asset classes, such as money market funds, bond mutual funds, and stock mutual funds. The percentages allocated to each class is dependent on your investment policy statement.

Mutual funds provide diversification because each fund holds numerous stocks and/or bonds. However, many mutual funds, based on their investment objective, hold many of the same type of stock or bond. Holding a particular mutual fund may provide diversification only in that sector or type of stock or bond.

Usually your portfolio does not become significantly more diversified by holding more than one or two large-cap stock funds or more than one or two government bond funds. Furthermore, your portfolio does become more diversified if you hold a small-cap, a mid-cap, and a large-cap fund; or if you hold a long-term corporate bond fund, a short-term government bond fund, and an international bond fund. Of course, the amount you purchase, if any, in the different types of funds is based on your Investment Policy Statement.

Therefore, selecting a mutual fund family that offers a fund in many of the different categories provides you with the ability to develop a well-diversified and properly allocated mutual fund portfolio. Thus, when you are reviewing the mutual fund groups, select only those that can offer you an adequate variety of funds from which to choose.

Other disadvantages of using many different mutual fund groups are:

- Difficulty of keeping track of all of your holdings and statements
- Difficulty and cost of transferring money from one fund group to another
- Knowing the shareholder services of each fund group
- Knowing the investment philosophy of each fund group

In order to select a well-diversified portfolio the mutual fund management group should offer at least one or two funds (or similar funds) from each category as shown in Figure 10.2.

Shareholder Services Provided

Shareholder services provide benefits to you in addition to the return from the mutual fund investment. Automatic investment plans, systematic withdrawal plans, consolidated statements, and exchange privileges are important to you in managing your portfolio efficiently (see Chapter 1).

Investment Professionals

Many investment professionals with brokerage firms or banks with brokerage operations may offer many different mutual fund groups. However, most investment professionals know a few groups in detail but not about all funds available. If the investment professional knows your Investment Policy Statement, he or she is able to recommend the appropriate group and more particularly the individual mutual funds for you. The investment professional many times knows the portfolio manager of the fund, has followed the fund's performance for many years, and is

Figure 10.2   Fund Types Available from a Mutual Fund Family

Growth Category*
Aggressive Growth Fund   Growth Fund
Small-Cap Growth Fund   Mid-Cap Growth Fund
Index Fund   Sector Fund—Various types

Growth and Income Category*
Large-Cap Fund   Growth and Income Fund
Total Return Fund   Value Fund
Utilities Fund   Balanced Fund

International Stock Category*
International Fund   International Region Fund
International Single Country Fund   Global Fund

Taxable Income Category*
Corporate Bond Fund–   Corporate Bond Fund–High Yield
  Investment Grade
Government Bond Fund   International Bond Fund
Global Bond Fund

Tax-exempt Income Category*
Tax-Exempt Bond Fund–National   Tax-Exempt Bond Fund–State

Money Market Category*
Money Market Fund

*Categories only include a limited number of representative funds and do not reflect a complete list of available funds. All funds may not be appropriate for you based on your investment policy statement.

knowledgeable about the shareholder services. When the stock or bond market fluctuates, you have an adviser to discuss your holding with to determine if any changes should be made. On the other hand, if someone tries to sell you an inappropriate fund he or she knows rather than finding the right fund for you, get a new adviser. Always research whether a potential adviser is reputable before using him or her.

Performance of the Funds

Not all mutual funds perform well during a given time period. Domestic stock funds may perform differently than international stock funds. Likewise, bond funds do not always perform the same as stock funds. However, large mutual fund management companies may at times have an advantage of hiring and using the nation's best portfolio managers. Furthermore, large management companies try very diligently to provide above-average returns. Their management companies are highlighted in most investment publications and a report of unhappy investors to an audience that wide is something they want to avoid.

Reputation of the Management Company

The reputation of the management company is important to you so that you know that the investment that you made is being managed properly and according to the prospectus. A good reputation attracts more capital to be managed, thus providing a reasonable profit from management fees to the mutual fund management company, which does not share in any profits from the fund's investments.

Cost Structure of the Funds

The cost structure of the mutual funds differs among family groups and even sometimes within the family of funds. Some mutual fund management groups offer different cost structures for each of their funds and some only offer one kind of structure. Do you want to buy shares with a front-end sales charge, a contingent deferred sales charge, or that are level-load or no-load? Typically, you may exchange within each family without a cost to you as long as the exchange takes place between funds with the same cost structure. If you want to sell shares from one family and buy shares in another family, you must decide if the added costs make that strategy worthwhile.

Ease of Placing an Order

Even though mutual funds are considered a long-term investment, the ease of placing an order may help you decide how you want to purchase mutual funds and from what financial institution. You may choose from:

- Telephoning or visiting your investment professional at a brokerage firm, a bank with brokerage operations, or a financial planning firm
- Calling the mutual fund management company directly
- Mailing your order directly to the mutual fund management company
- Placing an order over the Internet

Occasionally, time is of the essence when you are placing an order. You want to be able to get some advice from your investment professional and still place the order that same day.

Your Investment Policy Statement

Putting together all the information in this chapter, complete the following Your Investor's Guide–Your Investment Policy Statement.

Finally, Invest

Once you have prepared your investment policy statement–including asset allocation, mutual fund family, and individual mutual funds–it is time to invest. You may invest immediately or gradually over a period of time. Do whatever makes you most comfortable. Also, market conditions may influence as to when and how you should invest.

Investing is not a one-time event. You must continually review, re-evaluate, and adjust your investment policy statement and portfolio when appropriate.

Your Investor's Guide

Your Investment Policy Statement

Personal Information (complete the information)

Your Name _____

Your Spouse's Name _____

Address _____

Your Information		*Your Spouse's Information*
_____	Date of Birth	_____
_____	Social Security or Tax Identification Number	_____
_____	Home Telephone Number	_____
_____	Employer	_____
_____	Occupation	_____
_____	Business Telephone Number	_____

Type of Account (check the appropriate one)

❑ Individual   ❑ Retirement (IRA, SEP, or IRA Rollover)

❑ Joint   ❑ Other _____

❑ Trust

Author's Note: Knowing the type of account should assist you in selecting appropriate mutual funds for your portfolio.

Financial Condition (complete the information)

Income

Your Information		*Your Spouse's Information*
$_____	Annual Income	$_____

Your Investor's Guide (Continued)

Your Information	Assets	Your Spouse's Information
_____	Money Market Funds	_____
_____	Money Market Securities	_____
_____	Bond Mutual Funds	_____
_____	Other Bond Holdings	_____
_____	Stock Mutual Funds	_____
_____	Other Stock Holdings	_____
_____	Other Securities	_____
_____	Real Estate	_____
_____	Other Assets	_____
$_____	**Total Assets**	$_____

Your Information	Liabilities	Your Spouse's Information
_____	Mortgage(s)	_____
_____	Bank Loans	_____
_____	Credit Card Balances	_____
_____	Other Liabilities	_____
$_____	**Total Liabilities**	$_____
$_____	**Net Worth** **(Assets minus Liabilities)**	$_____

Author's Note: Knowing your financial condition may help you in determining your investment goals.

Investment Goals (number your goals in order of priority)

_____ Buy or build a home

_____ Higher standard of living

_____ Reduce dependence on employment income

_____ Start a new business

Your Investor's Guide (Continued)

Investment Goals (continued)

_____ College fund

_____ Travel and vacations

_____ Financial independence

_____ Substantial estate for heirs

_____ Retirement

_____ Other goal _____

_____ Other goal _____

_____ Other goal _____

_____ Other goal _____

Author's Note: Designating a dollar amount may aid you when selecting your investment goals.

Investment Objective (number your objectives in order of priority)

_____ Preservation of capital with some income

_____ Primarily income with capital appreciation second

_____ A balance between income and capital appreciation

_____ Primarily capital appreciation with income second

_____ Primarily capital appreciation with no consideration to income

Author's Note: Knowing and designating your investment objectives will help you select suitable mutual funds for your portfolio.

Risk Tolerance (mark the appropriate one)

_____ *Conservative.* You dislike risk and will invest in only the safest and highest quality investment to try to achieve a reasonable return.

_____ *Moderate.* You are willing to take some risk and will invest in medium-quality investments to try to achieve an above average return.

_____ *Aggressive.* You are willing to accept risk and will invest in low-quality investments to try to achieve a high return.

Author's Note: Your principal and income are at risk when investing in mutual funds. Determining your risk tolerance will help in selecting suitable funds for your portfolio.

Your Investor's Guide (Continued)

Expected Return (mark the appropriate one)

Your investment objective is to receive an average annual total return (including income and capital appreciation) of:

_____	3.0% to 5.0%	_____	11.1% to 13.0%
_____	5.1% to 7.0%	_____	13.1% to 15.0%
_____	7.1% to 9.0%	_____	more than 15.0%
_____	9.1% to 11.0%		

Author's Note: The greater potential return may mean greater potential risk to your principal and income.

Time Horizon to Accomplish Your: (write in each investment goal listed earlier, with its priority number, on the appropriate line)

_____	1 to 2 years
_____	3 to 4 years
_____	5 to 6 years
_____	7 to 8 years
_____	9 to 10 years
_____	11 to 12 years
_____	13 to 14 years
_____	15 to 16 years
_____	17 to 18 years
_____	19 to 20 years
_____	20 years plus

Author's Note: Your time horizon to accomplish each investment goal is a significant consideration when selecting the types of mutual funds for your portfolio.

Allocating Your Assets (designate your appropriate percent)

_____ % Money Market Funds

_____ % Bond Mutual Funds

_____ % Stock Mutual Funds

Author's Note: Allocating your assets may provide you with higher returns over the long term with less risk.

Your Investor's Guide (Continued)

Selecting Your Mutual Funds (list the mutual funds of each type that are suitable for you)

Money Market Fund

1. _____

Bond Mutual Funds

1. _____
2. _____
3. _____
4. _____
5. _____
6. _____

Stock Mutual Funds

1. _____
2. _____
3. _____
4. _____
5. _____
6. _____
7. _____
8. _____
9. _____
10. _____
11. _____
12. _____

Author's Note: The performance of your mutual fund is based on the performance of the underlying securities held in the fund.

Your Investor's Guide (Continued)

Measuring Your Returns (check the most appropriate one)

You want the performance returns of your portfolio to equal or exceed:

_____ Your investment objective

_____ An absolute number

_____ A risk-free investment

_____ A corresponding mutual fund index

_____ A corresponding market average or index

Author's Note: Measuring your fund's performance against specified benchmarks will help you assess your fund's performance. (See Chapter 18.)

Reviewing Your Investment Policy Statement and Portfolio (mark the appropriate one)

_____ I plan to do an annual review.

_____ I plan to do a semiannual review.

_____ I plan to do a quarterly review.

Author's Note: Reviewing—and revising, if necessary—your investment policy statement is important for you to achieve financial security.

CHAPTER 11

Allocating and Diversifying Your Assets

The two most important parts of your investment policy statement besides your investor's profile are allocating and diversifying your assets. Using allocation and diversification increases the probability that your portfolio will provide you with your expected return within your risk tolerance.

Allocation of Assets

Allocation of assets is an investment planning strategy whereby a portfolio is invested in money market funds, bond mutual funds, and stock mutual funds. Specific market categories react differently to changing economic environments. Each market has unique characteristics that mirror the investment climate of that category.

Bonds, money market securities, and stocks all react differently to each particular economic scenario. The percentages you invest in each type of fund are critical to meeting your investment expectations. Unfortunately, investor actions and reactions to economic predictions sometimes cause the markets to change contrary to normal accepted analysis.

Define Your Percentages

As discussed in Chapter 10, you have different levels of risk and return expectations. The percentages you specified for your serious money, investment money, and risk money (see Your Investors Guide—Types of Money in Chapter 10) help determine how to allocate your assets. If you specified a high percentage for your serious money, you might allocate more assets to money market funds. If you specified a high percentage for your investment money, you might allocate more assets to stock mutual funds and bond mutual funds. If you specified a high percentage for your risk money, you might allocate more assets to high-yield bond funds or aggressive growth stock funds. Of course, you must be comfortable about the percentages you select for the type of money and the asset allocation mix.

It usually is beneficial to diversify your assets within each market category by investing in several types of mutual funds. Depending on the amount of investable assets, you may not be able to efficiently invest in all categories. You may want to begin with only one or two categories with the idea of adding to the other one as you invest additional money. By allocating a certain percentage of your investment dollars to several different markets, the total return over time is generally more stable than if 100 percent of the dollars were invested in one market category, for example, stock mutual funds. Thus, a major downturn in one market will not significantly lower your total assets. (On the other hand, a major upturn in one market will not raise your total assets significantly either.)

Sample Asset Allocation Models

Portfolio models are infinite. There is no one correct model—even for people with the same goals, assets, and risk tolerances. Textbooks and software programs can lead you through many choices. Theoretical asset allocation models are a good place for you to begin the asset alloca-

FIGURE 11.1   Two Sample Asset Allocation Models Based on Three Investment Categories

Investment Objective: Capital Appreciation	Asset Category	Investment Objective: Income
60%	Stock Mutual Funds	30%
35	Bond Mutual Funds	60
5	Money Market Mutual Funds	10
100	Totals	100

tion process. Your asset allocation model should take into account your investor's profile you compiled in Chapter 10. You may feel comfortable in only one or two categories and not all three. Furthermore, you should only invest in asset categories that you believe are right for you and in which you are comfortable. Refer to Financial Focus 1 in Appendix B for a model portfolio allocation solely based on age.

Figure 11.1 displays two sample asset allocation models for investors whose investment objective is primarily income or primarily capital appreciation, based on the three traditional asset categories of money market mutual funds, bond mutual funds, and stock mutual funds. Most investors want some combination of both income and capital appreciation

Your Investor's Guide provides you with a table to designate your asset allocation among money market mutual funds, stock mutual funds, and bond mutual funds based on a primary investment objective of either capital appreciation or income.

Diversifying Your Assets

Diversification is an investment planning strategy that helps reduce risk by spreading investment dollars among market categories and among specific investments within each category. Each market category requires a different number of securities to be considered diversified.

Selection of a particular mutual fund is key because these investments will provide you with income, capital appreciation, or even a loss.

Your Investor's Guide

Your Asset Allocation Models Based on Three Investment Categories

Investment Objective: Capital Appreciation	Asset Category	Investment Objective: Income
___ %	Stock Mutual Funds	___ %
___ %	Bond Mutual Funds	___ %
___ %	Money Market Mutual Funds	___ %
100%	Totals	100%

Diversification relates directly to your investment objective. The mutual fund should be analyzed to determine if it is appropriate for your portfolio. When you are selecting a mutual fund, the investment manager of the fund has to be reviewed as well as the investment objective of the fund.

Investment professionals state that there is no such thing as a single ideal investment. Each investment has a unique composition, goal, and risk. Consider each of the following six investment characteristics to see how it fits with your investment objective:

1. Safety of principal
2. Income
3. Growth of income
4. Capital growth
5. Marketability
6. Tax benefits

One investment may have two or three of these characteristics, but generally none will have all six. Therefore, you should diversify among many different types of investments to try to achieve your overall investment objective, without assuming more risk than you can tolerate. A well-designed investment portfolio can offer you many characteristics of an ideal investment.

Difference Between Allocation and Diversification

The major difference between allocation and diversification is that allocation refers to the percentage of the portfolio invested in each security or market category, whereas, diversification usually refers to the number of securities or markets invested in.

Investment Characteristics

Each type of investment has certain characteristics, such as liquidity, volatility, and tax issues that you should consider when choosing investments.

Liquidity

Liquid investments can be converted quickly into cash to realize a gain, limit a loss, take advantage of another investment opportunity, or aid in an emergency. The amount of liquid investments you need depends in part on your individual circumstances such as your age, family situation, health, and wealth.

Volatility

Significant fluctuations in your principal value can occur in many investment areas. If you are not comfortable with volatility, you may want to consider an investment that does not fluctuate as much in value. However, you may exchange higher stability for lower returns. As stated before, mutual fund investments should be considered long term. If you have done your homework and chosen your funds wisely, you can avoid anxiety over volatility by reviewing your holdings periodically, such as monthly or quarterly and not every day.

Taxation

Taxes can affect the returns from an investment substantially. Appropriate tax and investment planning is always a goal. As with other trade-offs, you may invest in a fund that exposes you to higher taxation because its higher return still makes it an attractive fund. On the other hand, higher returns may push you into a higher tax bracket that lowers your net return.

It's Your Money, However...

You do not have to make all of your decisions about asset allocation and diversification by yourself. Your investment professional will give you insight on allocation of assets, management styles, performance figures, quality ratings, market outlook, and other investment information. Meeting with him or her on a regular basis will help you manage your portfolio better, and hopefully more profitably.

Some of the more sophisticated software programs also can help you make allocation and diversification decisions to best fit your investor's profile and your investment policy statement.

Make investment decisions for yourself. Evaluate the investments you own or are going to buy. Use the ideas and expertise of your professional or software package, but don't relinquish the final decision making to either.

Make your money work for you, so you don't have to work for your money! To achieve this goal, use your investment policy statement to form a broad strategy for how you want to allocate your assets and what diversification methods you want to use. Then your investment professional will help you analyze and determine the specific allocation and diversification for you. In the end, you must take responsibility for your investments. If the investment professional's recommendations do not seem to meet both your needs and objectives, you may want a second opinion, or even to choose a new adviser.

CHAPTER 12

Selecting Your Stock Mutual Funds

Now that you are using your investment policy statement, including your investor's profile, risk tolerance, expected return, and time horizon, select your mutual fund management company (family of funds) and the individual mutual funds. The funds you buy should fit into your overall portfolio's investment objective and meet your risk tolerance. Additionally, mutual funds are normally purchased for the long term. Timing short-term market swings is difficult. Therefore, funds that have performed steadily may do better over the long term than some of the more volatile funds.

Having a plan and defined objectives helps you avoid getting caught up in short-term popular investments. Rather than buying the "hot" funds of the year or the most publicized funds, match suitable funds to your investment objective(s). In many cases one year's "top performing funds" do not even survive until the next year's "top performing funds."

Even if you have only $1,000 to $2,000, you can still begin a mutual fund portfolio. Purchase one or two funds that meet your investment objective. (Because you did your homework, you don't have to sift through the more than 10,000 mutual funds, but can immediately look only at funds that meet your needs.) As you acquire more money, invest in different funds based on your asset allocation. Initially purchasing funds with high-quality securities may be your best approach. Build a foundation of funds with high-quality securities and then you may want to add funds that hold more aggressive securities. A small initial investment may become a significant amount over time.

Types of Stock Mutual Funds

Stock mutual funds may be broadly classified as domestic (United States) stock funds, international stock funds, and global stock funds. Investors purchase stock mutual funds primarily for capital appreciation and, in some funds, secondarily for income. Historically, these funds have generally provided good returns over the long term; however, they carry more risk of principal over the short term. Additionally, international and global stock mutual funds also carry currency risk.

Domestic (United States) Stock Funds

Domestic stock funds invest primarily in stocks of United States companies. Because many types of companies are traded in the marketplace, each prospectus will state the type of stocks the fund is allowed to purchase and the fund's investment objective.

Some of the more common types of domestic (United States) stock funds are:

- Large-cap growth stock fund
- Mid-cap growth fund
- Small-cap growth fund
- Growth and income fund
- Equity income fund
- Growth fund
- Aggressive growth fund
- Index fund
- Sector fund
- Theme fund

Large-cap growth fund. A large-capitalization (large-cap) growth fund invests in stocks of companies whose market capitalization is greater than $5 billion. Most of the companies are household names and have been in business for many years. Many of the companies do a substantial portion of their business outside of the United States. Most of the companies pay dividends and are considered high-quality investments. Another term commonly used to describe this type of company is *"blue chip."* Large-cap growth funds may also include *value funds* and *total return funds.*

Mid-cap growth fund. A mid-capitalization (mid-cap) growth fund invests in stocks of companies whose market capitalization is between $1 billion and $5 billion. Some of the companies are household names and have been in business for many years. Some of the companies in this classification do a portion of their business outside of the United States. Some of the companies pay dividends and are considered medium-quality investments. Mid-cap growth funds may be more volatile than large-cap growth funds.

Small-cap growth fund. A small-capitalization (small-cap) growth fund invests in stocks of companies whose market capitalization is less than $1 billion. Only a few of the companies are household names; many have been in business for only a relatively short time period. Some of the companies do a portion of their business outside of the United States. Most of the companies do not pay dividends and are considered more aggressive or lower quality investments. Small-cap growth funds may be more volatile than large-cap and mid-cap growth funds. Small-cap stock funds also are known as small company stock funds.

Multi-cap fund. A multi-capitalization (multi-cap) fund invests in stocks of large-cap, mid-cap, small-cap, and micro-cap companies. Companies with market capitalizations of less than $150 million are called *micro-cap* companies. Micro-cap companies may be very volatile due to the size of the company and the number of shares outstanding.

Growth and income fund. A growth and income fund invests in stocks of large-cap companies that have a history of paying and increasing dividends. Most of the companies are household names and have been in business for many years.

Equity income fund. An equity income fund invests in stocks of large, well-established companies that have a proven record of paying and increasing dividends. This fund also may invest in preferred stocks and convertible and nonconvertible bonds.

Total return fund. A total return fund invests primarily in large- and mid-cap stocks and in some cases bonds and preferred stocks. Many of the companies pay dividends and are considered high-quality investments. The fund concentrates on securities that may provide a high total return from both income and capital appreciation. Total return funds also may include growth and income funds and large-cap funds.

Value funds. A value fund invests primarily in large- and mid-cap stocks that are considered to be undervalued based on price-earnings ratios, price-book ratios, and market price relative to other similar companies. Many stocks also may have relatively high dividend yields.

Growth fund. A growth fund may invest in small-cap, mid-cap, and large-cap companies whose earnings growth potential may be superior. Growth funds also may invest in cyclical companies, depressed industries, turnaround situations, and other companies that appear to offer significant opportunities for long-term growth.

Aggressive growth fund. An aggressive growth fund, also known as a *capital appreciation* fund, invests in micro-cap, small-cap, and mid-cap companies. Furthermore, the fund invests in smaller, newer companies whose earnings growth potential may be superior. Aggressive growth funds also may invest in out-of-favor companies, cyclical companies, depressed industries, turnaround situations, and other companies that appear to offer significant opportunities for growth. The stocks in an aggressive growth fund are considered more risky and volatile than stocks in a growth or value fund.

Index fund. An index fund invests in stocks that represent a particular stock market index. The fund maintains the same stock positions that are used to compute the index. Some index funds use the same market capitalization for the stocks as the index uses to determine the number of shares held in the fund's portfolio. Under this calculation, a company with a large market capitalization will be represented more in the fund than a company with a small market capitalization.

Conversely, the fund may invest equal portions in all stocks that represent the index, rather than investing more in larger market-capitalization companies and less in smaller market-capitalization companies. The effect is that a smaller company has an equal impact on the performance of the fund as a larger company. Thus, the fund's performance may be similar to the index performance, but will vary depending on if the small-cap stocks are doing better or worse than the large-cap stocks.

The most common index used is the Standard & Poor's 500 Index. However, many other index funds are available that represent other stock indexes. Index mutual funds generally do not mirror exactly the respective index because mutual funds have fees and expenses; whereas, the index has no cost associated with its returns.

Strategic tax fund. A strategic tax fund invests in stocks and tax-exempt bonds to maximize the after-tax return of income and capital appreciation.

Sector fund. Sector funds invest in a portfolio of stocks of the same industry. *Sector* is used as another name for an industry. Stocks within a particular industry or sector will perform based on their own characteristics and fundamentals, in addition to the influence of the overall marketplace. Some sector funds will own stocks of several related industries, rather than stocks of just one industry. Sector funds may be either diversified or nondiversified. However, they usually carry more risk of principal than a broadly diversified fund because an industry may be significantly more volatile than the general market. Your selection of sector funds is numerous. Each mutual fund portfolio manager may classify each sector differently. Therefore, read the prospectus to determine which industries are being represented in the portfolio. Following are some of the more familiar sector funds with general descriptions.

Automobile. An automobile sector fund invests in stocks of companies whose primary business is manufacturing and selling automobiles, trucks, specialty vehicles, auto parts, and related services.

Brokerage. A brokerage sector fund invests in stocks of companies whose primary business is stock, bond, and commodity brokerage; investment banking; and investment management.

Building. A building sector fund invests in stocks of companies whose primary business is manufacturing, supplying, and distributing products and services related to the home building and home furnishing industries.

Chemical. A chemical sector fund invests in stocks of companies whose primary business is manufacturing, marketing, research, and related services to the chemical industry.

Communication. A communications sector fund invests in stocks of companies whose primary business is in telecommunication services and equipment.

Computer technology. A computer technology sector fund invests in stocks of companies whose primary business is designing, developing, manufacturing, and selling of products, processes, technologies, and services of computers and computer software.

Defense. A defense sector fund invests in stocks of companies whose primary business is designing, developing, manufacturing, and researching products and services of defense and aerospace industries.

Electronic. An electronic sector fund invests in stocks of companies whose primary business is designing, manufacturing, and selling electronic equipment and electronic components.

Energy. An energy sector fund invests in stocks of companies whose primary business is the production and distribution of oil, natural gas, coal, electricity, and other sources of energy.

Energy service. An energy service sector fund invests in stocks of companies whose primary business is providing equipment, electronic services, and other related products and services to the energy companies.

Food. A food sector fund invests in stocks of companies whose primary business is manufacturing, selling, and processing food and food products.

Health science. A health science sector fund invests in stocks of companies whose primary business is researching, manufacturing, selling, and delivering products and services of health care, drugs, and medicine.

Industrial equipment. An industrial equipment chemical sector fund invests in stocks of companies whose primary business is manufacturing and selling industrial equipment and products.

Insurance. A insurance sector fund invests in stocks of companies whose primary business is underwriting; reinsuring; and selling life, property, casualty, and health insurance.

Leisure. A leisure sector fund invests in stocks of companies whose primary business is designing, manufacturing, selling, and providing products and services for the leisure industry.

Multimedia. A multimedia sector fund invests in stocks of companies whose primary business is producing and distributing products and services for the broadcasting, media, and film industry.

Paper and forest products. A paper and forest products sector fund invests in stocks of companies whose primary business is researching, manufacturing, and selling paper and forest products.

Precious metal. A precious metal sector fund invests in stocks of companies whose primary business is exploring, mining, processing, and selling gold, silver, platinum, and other precious metals and minerals.

Real estate. A real estate sector fund invests in stocks of companies whose primary business is mortgage lending and constructing real estate.

Transportation. A transportation sector fund invests in stocks of two categories of companies: those who move people and goods, and those who design, manufacture, and sell services and products for aircraft, trucks, railroads, and other transportation equipment.

Utility. A utility sector fund invests in stocks of companies whose primary business is providing electric, gas, telephone, water, and related services to industrial, commercial, and residential communities. Because the utility sector is very large with numerous companies, utility funds are usually categorized as a major mutual fund category rather than just a sector fund category.

Typically, utility stock funds are less volatile than growth and value funds. They also provide a higher level of income than growth and value funds. Shares of utility stock funds usually change in price based on interest rate changes, in addition to companies' earnings, dividends, regulatory environment, and other market factors.

Theme fund. Theme funds are very similar to sector funds. However, the portfolio manager selects stocks of companies that are related to the theme, but that are not necessarily of the same industry. Investing in several theme funds provides broad diversification over many industries. Some of the more common types of theme funds are:

- Consumer products and services fund
- Environmental fund
- Financial services fund
- Information fund
- Natural resources fund
- Social and lifestyle fund

Consumer products and services. A consumer products and services theme fund invests in stocks of companies whose primary business is manufacturing, marketing, and retailing consumer products and services.

Environmental. An environmental theme fund invests in stocks of companies whose primary business is pollution control, waste management, and other environment-related services.

Financial services. A financial services theme fund invests in stocks of companies whose primary business is banking, mortgage lending, consumer lending, securities trading, and other financial services.

Information. An information theme fund invests in stocks of companies whose primary business is researching, manufacturing, and selling products, components, and services for the telephone, television, radio, computer, software, and other electronic data transmission industries.

Natural resources. A natural resources theme fund invests in stocks of companies whose primary business is exploring, developing, owning, and distributing oil, gas, coal, metals, and other natural resources.

Social and lifestyle. A social and lifestyle theme fund invests in stocks of companies whose primary business is based on the current and/or future trends of consumers' lifestyles and priorities.

International Stock Funds

International stock funds (also known as *foreign* stock funds) invest primarily in stocks of international (foreign) companies. An international stock mutual fund investment objective is usually capital appreciation. Some of the more common types of international stock funds are:

- International growth fund
- International large-cap growth fund
- International mid-cap growth fund
- International small-cap growth fund
- Emerging markets fund
- Foreign country fund
- Foreign region fund

In addition to other risks, international (foreign) stock funds carry currency risk (see Chapter 3).

International growth fund. An international growth fund may invest in small-cap, mid-cap, and large-cap foreign companies. International funds also may invest in cyclical companies, depressed industries, turnaround situations, and other companies that appear to offer significant opportunities for long-term growth. In addition to other risks, international stock funds carry currency risk.

International large-cap growth fund. An international large-cap growth fund invests in stocks of foreign companies whose market capitalization is greater than $5 billion. Most of the companies are foreign household names and many are household names to you. They are considered high-quality investments. In addition to other risks, international large-cap stock funds carry currency risk.

International mid-cap growth fund. An international mid-cap growth fund invests in stocks of foreign companies whose market capitalization is between $1 billion and $5 billion. Some of the companies are foreign household names but may be unknown to you. The companies are considered medium-quality investments. In addition to other risks, international mid-cap stock funds carry currency risk.

International small-cap growth fund. An international small-cap growth fund invests in stocks of foreign companies whose market capitalization is less than $1 billion. Only a few of the companies are foreign household names and very few may be familiar to you. Most of the companies do not pay dividends and are considered more aggressive or lower quality investments. In addition to other risks, international small-cap stock funds carry currency risk. Small-cap stock funds also are known as *small company stock funds.*

Emerging markets fund. An emerging markets fund invests in stocks of foreign companies whose country is less developed than a more economically-advanced country. Investments in stocks of companies in these countries pose significantly more risk due to lack of market liquidity, less reliable financial information, less stability politically and economically, and lack of substantial capital infrastructure. In addition to other risks, emerging markets funds carry currency risk.

Foreign country fund. An international foreign single country fund may invest in small-cap, mid-cap, and large-cap companies of one particular foreign country. However, the fund invests in companies whose earnings growth potential may be superior, or whose stock is considered undervalued. International foreign country funds also may invest in cyclical companies, depressed industries, turnaround situations, and other companies who appear to offer significant opportunities for long-term growth. In addition to other risks, foreign country stock funds carry currency risk.

Foreign region fund. An international foreign region fund may invest in small-cap, mid-cap, and large-cap foreign companies of a particular geographical region. The region may consist of two or more foreign countries. However, the fund usually invests in foreign companies whose earnings growth potential may be superior, or whose stock is considered undervalued. International foreign region funds also may invest in cyclical companies, depressed industries, turnaround situations, and other companies who appear to offer significant opportunities for long-term growth. In addition to other risks, foreign region stock funds carry currency risk.

Global Stock Funds

Global stock funds purchase stocks of companies throughout the world. This fund gives you more diversification than a single foreign country fund or a foreign region fund because it buys both United States and international stocks. Global stock mutual funds' investment objectives are typically capital appreciation. Some of the more common types of global stock funds are:

- Global fund
- Global large-cap growth fund
- Global mid-cap growth fund
- Global small-cap growth fund
- Global utility fund

In addition to other risks, global stock funds carry currency risk.

Global fund. A global stock fund may invest in small-cap, mid-cap, and large-cap United States and foreign companies. Typically the fund invests in large, well-established United States and foreign companies whose earnings growth potential may be superior. Global funds also may invest in cyclical companies, depressed industries, and turnaround situations and other companies who appear to offer significant opportunities for long-term growth. In addition to other risks, global funds carry currency risk.

Global large-cap growth fund. A global large-cap growth fund invests in stocks of both United States and foreign companies whose market capitalization is greater than $5 billion. Most of the companies are household names and are considered high-quality investments. In addition to other risks, global large-cap stock funds carry currency risk.

Global mid-cap growth fund. A global mid-cap growth fund invests in stocks of both United States and foreign companies whose market capitalization is between $1 billion and $5 billion. Some of the companies are foreign household names but may be unknown to you. The companies are considered medium-quality investments. In addition to other risks, global mid-cap stock funds carry currency risk.

Global small-cap growth fund. A global small-cap growth fund invests in stocks of both United States and foreign companies whose market capitalization is less than $1 billion. Only a few of the companies are foreign household names and very few may be familiar to you. Most of the companies do not pay dividends and are consider'ed more aggressive or lower quality investments. In addition to other risks, global small-cap stock funds carry currency risk. Global small-cap stock funds also are known as *global small company stock funds.*

Global utility fund. A global utility fund invests in stocks of companies whose primary business is providing electric, gas, telephone, water, and related services to industrial, commercial, and residential communities. In addition to other risks, global utility stock funds carry currency risk.

CHAPTER 13

Selecting Your Bond Mutual Funds

Bond Mutual Funds

In addition to investing in stock mutual funds, you might want to consider bond mutual funds. You can choose from several categories, such as U.S. bond funds, international bond funds, and global bond funds. Purchased primarily for income, bond mutual fund categories include government, municipal, and corporate bond funds. The basic risks associated with bond funds are credit risk and interest rate risk. International and global bond funds also carry currency risk.

Domestic (U.S.) Bond Funds

Domestic (U.S.) bond funds primarily purchase bonds issued by entities in the United States. Each fund typically buys bonds or notes of a particular range of maturities, that is, short-term, intermediate-term, or long-term. Within each of these categories, the fund can be classified as high-quality, medium-quality, or low-quality. U.S. bond funds also can be classified as taxable or tax-exempt. *Taxable bond funds* invest in bonds that pay taxable interest income, such as corporate and U.S. government bonds. *Tax-exempt bond funds* invest in bonds that pay tax-exempt interest income, such as municipal bonds. Some funds invest only in municipal bonds issued by one particular state to obtain the tax benefits of that state.

Taxable U.S. bond funds. Some of the more common types of taxable U.S. bond funds are:

- U.S. Government bond fund
- U.S. Treasury bond fund
- GNMA bond fund
- Adjustable-rate mortgage fund
- Corporate long-term bond fund
- Corporate intermediate-term bond fund
- Corporate short-term bond fund
- Investment-grade corporate bond fund
- Convertible securities fund
- High-yield bond fund
- Target maturity fund

U.S. government bond fund. A U.S. government bond fund invests in bonds and notes issued both by the United States and its federal agencies. However, U.S. government bond funds are neither guaranteed by nor obligations of the U.S. government.

U.S. Treasury bond fund. A U.S. Treasury bond fund invests in bonds and notes issued only by the U.S. Treasury. However, U.S. Treasury bond funds are neither guaranteed by nor obligations of the U.S. government.

GNMA bond fund. A GNMA bond fund invests in bonds issued by the Government National Mortgage Association, a federal agency of the United States. GNMA (also known as Ginnie Mae) bonds are backed by the full faith and credit of the U.S. government. However, GNMA bond funds are neither guaranteed by nor obligations of the United States government nor any agency thereof.

Adjustable-rate mortgage (ARM) fund. An adjustable-rate mortgage fund invests in adjustable-rate mortgage bonds and floating-rate notes.

Corporate long-term bond fund. A corporate long-term bond fund invests in bonds issued by corporations. Generally, the bonds have maturities of more than ten years. The fund's prospectus explains in detail the ratings of bonds the fund is allowed to purchase. However, the bonds usually are considered investment grade.

Corporate intermediate-term bond fund. A corporate intermediate-term bond fund invests in bonds and notes issued by corporations. Generally, the bond and notes have maturities of ten years or less. The fund's prospectus explains in more detail the ratings of bonds the fund is allowed to purchase. However, the bonds and notes usually are considered investment grade.

Corporate short-term bond fund. A corporate short-term bond fund invests in bonds and notes issued by corporations. Generally, the bond and notes have maturities of five years or less. The fund's prospectus explains in more detail the ratings of bonds the fund is allowed to purchase. However, the bonds and notes usually are considered investment grade.

Convertible securities fund. A convertible securities fund invests in convertible bonds and convertible preferred stock issued by corporations. Generally, the bonds have maturities of 20 years or less, and preferred stock has no maturities. The fund's prospectus explains in more detail the ratings of bonds and preferred stock the fund is allowed to purchase. However, the bonds and preferred stock usually are considered to be medium to lower grade.

High-yield bond fund. A high-yield or high-income bond fund invests in bonds and notes issued by corporations. Generally, the bonds have maturities of 20 years or less. The fund's prospectus explains in more detail the ratings of bonds the fund is allowed to purchase. However, the bonds and notes are considered medium to lower grade that carry greater risk than investment-grade bonds. High-yield or high-income bonds are commonly known as *junk bonds.*

Target maturity fund. A target maturity fund invests in zero-coupon U.S. Treasury securities, mortgage-backed securities, and other zero-coupon securities with a specific maturity date coinciding with the liquidation of the fund.

Tax-exempt U.S. bond fund. Some of the more common types of tax-exempt U.S. bond funds are:

- National municipal bond fund—investment grade (long-term, intermediate-term, and short-term)
- National municipal bond fund—high yield
- Single state municipal bond fund

National municipal bond fund—investment grade (long-term). A long-term national municipal bond fund invests in investment-grade, tax-exempt bonds with maturities of longer than ten years. The mutual fund only holds investment-grade bonds, that is, bonds rated Baa3 or higher by Moody's and BBB– or higher by S&P, and any nonrated bond considered by the portfolio manager to be of equal quality.

National municipal bond fund—investment grade (intermediate-term). An intermediate-term national municipal bond fund invests in investment-grade, tax-exempt bonds with maturities of three to ten years. The mutual fund only holds investment-grade bonds, that is, bonds rated Baa3 or higher by Moody's and BBB– or higher by S&P, and any nonrated bond considered by the portfolio manager to be of equal quality.

National municipal bond fund—investment grade (short-term). A short-term national municipal bond fund invests in investment-grade, tax-exempt bonds with maturities of less than three years. The mutual fund only holds investment-grade bonds, that is, bonds rated Baa3 or higher by Moody's and BBB– or higher by S&P, and any nonrated bond considered by the portfolio manager to be of equal quality.

National municipal bond fund—high yield. A long-term national high-yield municipal bond fund typically invests in noninvestment-grade, tax-exempt bonds with maturities of longer than ten years. The mutual fund primarily holds noninvestment-grade bonds, that is, bonds rated Ba1 or lower by Moody's and BB+ or lower by S&P. A high-yield bond fund is also known as a *high-income fund.*

Single state municipal bond fund. A single state municipal bond fund invests in tax-exempt bonds issued by one particular state. Most funds purchase investment-grade bonds.

International Bond Funds

International bond funds (also known as a foreign bond funds) purchase primarily bonds issued outside of the United States, such as bonds of foreign corporations and foreign governments. The fund also may be classified as short-term, intermediate-term, or long-term, depending on the fund's investment objective. In addition to other risks, an international bond fund carries currency risk.

Some of the more common types of international (foreign) bond funds are:

- International government bond fund
- International corporate bond fund
- Foreign country bond fund
- Foreign region bond fund

International government bond fund. An international government bond fund invests in bonds issued by foreign governments. However, international government bond funds are neither guaranteed by nor obligations of the respective foreign governments.

International corporate bond fund. An international corporate bond fund invests in bonds issued by foreign corporations.

Foreign country bond fund. A foreign country bond fund invests in bonds issued by corporations and the government of a single foreign country.

Foreign region bond fund. A foreign region bond fund invests in bonds issued by corporations and governments of several foreign countries, usually with a close geographical proximity.

Global Bond Funds

A global bond fund purchases bonds of companies and governments throughout the world. A global fund gives you more diversification than a one-country or foreign region fund because it buys both United States and international bonds. In addition to other risks, a global bond fund carries currency risk.

Some of the more common types of global bond funds are:

- Global government bond fund
- Multi-sector bond fund
- World income bond fund
- Short-term world income fund
- Emerging markets bond fund

Global government bond fund. A global government bond fund invests in bonds issued by the United States and foreign governments. However, global government bond funds are neither guaranteed by nor obligations of their respective governments.

Multi-sector bond fund. A multi-sector bond fund purchases primarily bonds that are issued by the U.S. government and corporations, and foreign governments and corporations. The fund also may be classified as short-term, intermediate-term, or long-term, depending on the fund's investment objective. Some multi-sector bond funds also purchase high-yield (low-rated) bonds.

World income bond fund. Similar to a multi-sector bond fund, a world income bond fund purchases bonds issued by governments and corporations of economically developed countries. The bonds typically have long-term maturities.

Short-term world income fund. A short-term world income fund purchases notes issued by the governments and corporations of economically developed countries. The notes have short-term maturities.

Emerging markets bond fund. An emerging markets bond fund purchases bonds issued by the U.S. government and corporations, and foreign governments and corporations of economically less developed countries.

CHAPTER 14

Other Types of Funds

In addition to stock and bond funds, you may want to consider some other types of funds, such as money market funds, balanced funds, and asset allocation funds.

Money Market Funds

A *money market fund* purchases money market securities. *Money market securities* are short-term (maturities of one year or less) debt obligations with high liquidity. *Liquidity* means an investment may be converted to cash quickly and easily. Most money market funds primarily hold underlying securities that mature within 90 days. The price of the fund is $1 per share. The price typically does not vary, although the fund cannot guarantee that the price will not change. Redeeming your shares of your money market fund readily to cash provides you with liquidity. You normally earn dividends daily, and they may be paid to your account monthly. The dividend yield can fluctuate based on changes of the short-term interest rates and the securities held in the fund's portfolio.

Brokerage firms' money market funds. Most brokerage firms' money market funds are not insured by the Federal Deposit Insurance

Corporation (FDIC) or the Securities Investor Protection Corporation (SIPC). Nonetheless, their safety as investments for preservation of principal is high.

Benefits of money market funds. Money market funds provide liquidity, safety of principal, and current income. They may be used as reserve funds for your money while you decide where to invest next.

How money market funds are classified. Money market funds offer either taxable or tax-exempt dividends, depending on the underlying securities held in the portfolio.

Taxable money market funds. *Regular* money market funds invest in short-term securities, such as U.S. Treasury bills and notes, commercial paper, and certificates of deposit (CDs). *Government* money market funds typically invest in U.S. Treasury and federal agency securities.

Tax-exempt money market funds. *Municipal* money market funds invest in short-term municipal notes. The dividends received are exempt from federal income taxation.

Money Market Deposit Accounts

A *money market deposit account* (MMDA) offered by a bank or savings institution is not the same as a money market fund offered by a brokerage firm or by a bank with brokerage operations. Specifically, the yields and your ability to make withdrawals from money market deposit accounts differ, depending on the financial institutions. Money market deposit accounts are insured by the FDIC.

Some brokerage firms offer insured money market deposit accounts. If your objective is safety of principal, consider investing a portion of your assets in an insured money market deposit account. Before investing in either a money market mutual fund or a money market deposit account, compare the differences between them, including the rates of return, liquidity, and safety of each.

Balanced Mutual Funds

Purchased primarily for capital appreciation and moderate income, balanced mutual funds invest in stocks and bonds. Balanced funds also may purchase money market securities. The types of stocks and bonds vary, depending on a fund's investment objective. The percentage invested in each category also varies depending on the portfolio manager's market allocation and the restrictions set forth in the prospectus. The basic risks associated with balanced funds are risk of principal, credit risk, and interest rate risk. International and global balanced funds also carry currency risk.

Some of the more common types of balanced funds are:

- Balanced growth fund
- Balanced income fund
- Balanced international fund
- Balanced global fund

Balanced growth fund. A balanced growth fund invests in both stocks and bonds, with a larger proportion in stocks than in bonds. The quality and type of bonds and stocks are dependent on the investment objective set forth in the prospectus.

Balanced income fund. A balanced income fund invests in both stocks and bonds, with an larger proportion in bonds than in stocks. The quality and type of bonds and stocks are dependent on the investment objective set forth in the prospectus.

Balanced international fund. A balanced international fund invests in both stocks of foreign corporations and bonds of foreign corporations and governments. The quality and type of bonds and stocks are dependent on the investment objective set forth in the prospectus. The allocation of bonds and stocks is also dependent on the investment objective(s) of the fund.

Balanced global fund. A balanced global fund invests in both stocks of domestic and foreign corporations and in bonds of domestic and foreign corporations and governments. The quality and type of bonds and stocks are dependent on the investment objective set forth in the prospectus. The allocation of bonds and stocks also are dependent on the investment objective of the fund. The fund's prospectus may limit the percent that may be invested in foreign and United States securities.

Asset Allocation Mutual Funds

Purchased primarily for total return, asset allocation mutual funds invest in stocks, bonds, and money market securities. One such feature of the fund is flexibility of the percent allocated to stocks, bonds, and money market securities. The fund may shift all or most of its assets into one type of security, such as all stocks or all bonds or all money market securities. The portfolio manager usually uses an asset allocation model to time the market. This helps him or her decide when to shift the assets from one category to another. *Market timing* is the technique of trying to buy low and sell high rather than staying fully invested for the long-term. The typical investment objective of an asset allocation fund is capital appreciation. The basic risks associated with the funds are risk of principal, credit risk, and interest rate risk.

Most asset allocation funds maintain a relatively constant percent of stocks, bonds, and money market securities and shifts in the allocation are gradual.

Some of the more common types of asset allocation funds are:

- Asset allocation domestic fund
- Asset allocation international fund
- Asset allocation global fund

Asset allocation domestic fund. An asset allocation domestic fund invests in domestic stocks, bonds, and money market securities. The quality and type of bonds and stocks are dependent on the investment objective set forth in the prospectus. The percent allocation of stocks, bonds, and money market securities is usually based on the portfolio manager's market outlook.

Asset allocation international fund. An asset allocation international fund invests in international (foreign) stocks, bonds, and money market securities. The quality and type of bonds and stocks are dependent on the investment objective set forth in the prospectus. The percent allocation of stocks, bonds, and money market securities is usually based on the portfolio manager's market outlook.

Asset allocation global fund. An asset allocation global fund invests in both domestic (United States) and international (foreign) stocks, bonds, and money market securities. The quality and type of bonds and stocks are dependent on the investment objective set forth in the prospectus. The percent allocation of stocks, bonds, and money market securities is usually based on the portfolio manager's market outlook.

CHAPTER 15

Using Mutual Fund Wrap Accounts

Several brokerage firms and mutual fund companies offer wrap accounts as a method to purchase individual mutual funds. Wrap accounts are also known as *mutual fund asset allocation programs.* A *wrap account,* sometimes called a *wrap program,* provides an advisory service for you to have your assets continuously invested among a group of mutual funds. You may pay one annual fee, which normally ranges from 0 percent to a maximum of 1.5 percent for the service. The wrap fee covers the determination of how assets are to be allocated, buying and selling the funds, portfolio rebalancing, advisory services, and performance monitoring. Additional fees that may be charged to the fund's assets include management fees, administrative fees, 12b-1 distribution fees, custodial fees, commissions, and other operating expenses. Brokerage firms and mutual fund companies who offer wrap accounts are referred to as *sponsors.*

In Chapter 10, the need for and importance of preparing your *investment policy statement* is discussed. The seven steps to formulate and adhere to your investment policy statement are:

1. Prepare your investor's profile.
2. Understand your risks and returns.
3. Allocate your assets.
4. Select your mutual funds.
5. Measure your risks and returns.
6. Monitor your mutual fund's performance.
7. Review your portfolio and investment policy statement.

Prior to investing in a mutual fund wrap account, you usually complete a questionnaire to identify your investment objectives, risk tolerance, and suitability of types of mutual funds. Mutual fund wrap accounts attempt to provide a method for you to create and implement an investment policy statement and allocate your assets among several different types of mutual funds. Using a wrap account allows you (or the sponsor) to perform the necessary steps to construct a diversified investment portfolio of mutual funds and monitor their performance on a regular basis. The number of funds available to you is different for each sponsor's wrap account. However, the selection can range from as little as ten funds to as many as several hundred. Your investment professional should be able to assist you in completing the questionnaire and explaining the fees, structure, and other features of a wrap account.

Wrap accounts are categorized as portfolio of investment trusts, portfolio of proprietary family of funds, and portfolio of multiple family of funds.

Portfolio of Investment Trusts

A wrap account offered by a sponsor, structured as a portfolio of investment trusts, usually uses funds that are managed by institutional portfolio managers. The portfolio management is generally nondiscretionary, whereby you select your own asset allocation or formally accept the asset allocation recommendation from your investment professional (sponsoring brokerage firm) or sponsoring mutual fund company. However, some wrap accounts may be discretionary. *Discretionary* means that the sponsor or portfolio manager may buy or sell your mutual fund shares *without* getting your prior approval. However, you will receive notice of the transaction within a few days of the trade. Monthly or quarterly statements show all of the activity.

The account is monitored monthly or quarterly with appropriate recommendations to rebalance the portfolio of funds. *Rebalancing* means that a portion of some funds are sold and the proceeds are used to purchase shares of existing funds to adjust the percent back to the original percent allocation. This is done in each category of money market funds, bond funds, and stock funds. Rebalancing also may mean adjusting the portfolio to the original percent allocated to each type of fund held based on the fund's investment objective such as growth, aggressive growth, income, etc. The funds also may be rebalanced according to domestic and international funds, if you selected foreign funds.

In addition to the wrap fee, you may pay additional fees that are charged against the fund's net assets. Some of the additional fees are management fees, administrative fees, 12b-1 distribution fees, and other expenses.

Portfolio of Proprietary Family of Funds

A wrap account offered by a sponsor, structured as a portfolio of proprietary family of funds, uses funds managed by the sponsor's mutual fund company or its affiliate. The portfolio management is generally discretionary, whereby you accept the asset allocation recommendation from your investment professional (sponsoring brokerage firm) or sponsoring mutual fund company. The account is monitored monthly or quarterly with appropriate rebalancing of the portfolio's funds according to its objectives.

In addition to the wrap fee, if any, you may pay additional fees that are charged against the fund's net assets. Some of the additional fees are management fees, administrative fees, 12b-1 distribution fees, and other expenses.

Portfolio of Multiple Family of Funds

With wrap fee. A wrap account offered by a sponsor, structured as a portfolio of multiple family of funds, uses funds managed by the sponsor's mutual fund company, its affiliate, or a nonaffiliate. The portfolio management is generally discretionary, whereby you accept the asset allocation recommendation from your investment professional (sponsoring brokerage firm) or sponsoring mutual fund company. The account is monitored monthly or quarterly with appropriate rebalancing of the portfolio's funds according to its objectives.

In addition to the wrap fee, you may pay additional fees that are charged against the fund's net assets. Some of the additional fees are management fees, administrative fees, 12b-1 distribution fees, and other expenses.

Without wrap fee. A wrap account offered by a sponsor, structured as a portfolio of multiple family of funds, usually uses funds managed by the sponsor's mutual fund company, its affiliate, or a nonaffiliate. The portfolio management is generally nondiscretionary, whereby you select your own asset allocation or formally accept the asset allocation recommendation from the sponsoring brokerage firm or mutual fund company. The account is monitored and reported to you monthly or quarterly so you may rebalance the portfolio's funds.

You do not pay a wrap fee or transaction fees for buying and selling the mutual funds' shares. However, the funds you own may be charged a participation fee for belonging to the sponsor's wrap program account. The participation fee is charged to the fund's net assets.

CHAPTER 16

Measuring Your Risks and Returns

There are two basic rules of investing:

1. Make money.
2. Don't lose money.

It sounds simple, but in an attempt to make money in the stock and bond market, whether it be through mutual funds, individual securities, or other types of investment vehicles, the possibility of losing money is always present. Therefore, the overriding objective is to make the most money with the least loss. In investment terms, this objective is called risk versus return. How much risk must you take to pursue a certain return? Determining the potential risk and the potential return from investments made in the stock and bond markets is very difficult to know.

Ratings and Rankings of the Underlying Securities

Money market securities, bonds, and stocks are rated and ranked by independent research firms. The two primary research firms are *Standard & Poor's (S&P)* and *Moody's Investors Service (Moody's)*.

Money Market Securities

Moody's rates short-term debt obligations, which are considered money market securities. The ratings are Moody's opinions of the ability of issuers to punctually repay senior debt obligations that have an original maturity not exceeding one year. Obligations relying on support mechanisms such as letters of credit and bonds of indemnity are excluded unless explicitly rated. Moody's employs three designations, all judged to be investment grade, to indicate the relative repayment ability of rated issues. Figure 16.1 shows Moody's short-term debt ratings.

Bonds and Notes

When you are contemplating buying a bond or note, its credit rating should be one of the main considerations. Bonds are rated by *Standard & Poor's* on the issuer's perceived ability to pay the interest and principal at maturity. Bonds and notes are rated by *Moody's* on an assessment of both the likelihood that the issuer will default (i.e., miss payments) on a security, and the amount of loss if a default occurs.

Taxable bonds. Bonds and notes rated as being *investment grade* have one of the four highest ratings. Bonds and notes rated below this level are considered low quality and are sometimes referred to as "junk" bonds, which means that they carry more risk and more potential for volatility. *Junk bonds* are also known as *high-yield bonds*.

Tax-exempt bonds. Some municipal bonds and notes are insured by an insurance company that guarantees the timely payment of all principal and interest on a municipal bond should the issuer default. Some of the well-known municipal bond insurers are: AMBAC Indemnity Corporation (AMBAC), Financial Guaranty Insurance Company (FGIC), Financial Security Assurance (FSA), and Municipal Bond Investors Assurance (MBIA). Insured bonds generally earn an Aaa rating by Moody's or AAA by S&P.

Uninsured bonds are rated by Moody's and S&P based on the companies' regular criteria.

FIGURE 16.1 Moody's Short-Term Debt Ratings

Rating	Description
Prime-1	Issuers have *superior ability* for repayment of senior short-term debt obligations.
Prime-2	Issuers have a *strong ability* for repayment of senior short-term debt obligations.
Prime-3	Issuers have an *acceptable ability* for repayment of senior short-term debt obligations.
Not Prime	Issuers do not fall within any of the Prime rating categories.

Source: Used by permission of Moody's Investors Service, Inc.

When you are selecting a bond mutual fund, consider these ratings for the portfolio's underlying bonds and notes. Figure 16.2 shows Moody's and S&P's ratings for corporate and municipal bonds.

Consult *Standard & Poor's Bond Guide* and *Moody's Annual Bond Record* and *Moody's Global Ratings Guide* for international bonds for expanded definitions for each rating category. See Appendix D for addresses.

Common Stocks

When analyzing a stock, you may use rankings to determine the quality of the company. Both S&P and Moody's rank stocks based on stability of earnings and record of dividend payments. The ranking is an evaluation of past stability of earnings and dividend payments, not a recommendation or a prediction of future market price.

Standard & Poor's ranks common stocks according to the following designations:

A+ Highest	B+ Average	C Lowest
A High	B Below Average	D In Reorganization
A– Above Average	B– Lower	NR No Ranking

Figure 16.2   Moody's and S&P Corporate and Municipal Bond Ratings

Moody's	Definitions	Standard & Poor's
Aaa	Highest quality	AAA
Aa	High quality	AA
A	Good quality	A
Baa	Adequate quality	BBB
Ba	Speculative	BB
B	Speculative	B
Caa, Ca, C	Speculative	CCC, CC, C
NR	Not rated	NR
	Default	D

The ratings from Aa to B may be modified by a "1, 2, or 3," where 1 is highest and 3 is lowest.
The ratings from AA to CCC may be modified by a "+" or "–," where + is highest and – is lowest.

Source: Used by permission of Moody's Investors Service, Inc. Reprinted by permission of Standard & Poor's, a division of The McGraw-Hill Companies.

Moody's grades stocks according to the following designations:

High Grade	Medium Grade
Investment Grade	Lower Medium Grade
Upper Medium Grade	Speculative Grade

Source: Reprinted by permission of Standard & Poor's, a division of The McGraw-Hill Companies. Used by permission of Moody's Investors Service, Inc.

See *Standard & Poor's Stock Guide* and *Moody's Handbook of Common Stocks* for further explanation of the rankings. See Appendix D for addresses.

Ratings and Rankings of Mutual Funds

Several research firms rate and rank mutual funds primarily based on quality, past performance, risk, and expected return. Moody's, Morningstar, Standard & Poor's, and Value Line are some of the better-known research firms that offer mutual fund ratings and rankings.

Figure 16.3   Moody's Bond Mutual Fund Ratings

Rating	Description
Aaa	Funds are judged to be of an investment quality similar to Aaa-rated fixed income obligations, that is, they are judged to be of the best quality.
Aa	Funds are judged to be of an investment quality similar to Aa-rated fixed income obligations, that is, they are judged to be of high quality by all standards.
A	Funds are judged to be of an investment quality similar to A-rated fixed income obligations, that is, they are judged to possess many favorable investment attributes and are considered as upper-medium-grade investment vehicles.
Baa	Funds are judged to be of an investment quality similar to Baa-rated fixed income obligations, that is, they are considered as medium-grade investment vehicles.
Ba	Funds are judged to be of an investment quality similar to Ba-rated fixed income obligations, that is, they are judged to have speculative elements.
B	Funds are judged to be of an investment quality similar to B-rated fixed income obligations, that is, they generally lack characteristics of the desirable investment.

Source: Used by permission of Moody's Investors Service, Inc. See *Moody's Money Market and Bond Fund Ratings* for a further explanation of the ratings.

Moody's Investors Service. The ratings are Moody's opinions about the investment quality of shares in bond mutual funds that principally invest in short-term and long-term fixed-income obligations. As such, the ratings incorporate Moody's assessment of a fund's published investment objective and policies, the creditworthiness of the assets held by the fund, and the management characteristics of the fund. The ratings are not intended to predict performance of a fund with respect to appreciation, volatility of net asset value, or yield. Figure 16.3 shows Moody's mutual fund ratings.

FIGURE 16.4　Morningstar Mutual Fund Ratings

Rating	Description
☆☆☆☆☆	Highest Rating
☆☆☆☆	Above Average Rating
☆☆☆	Average Rating
☆☆	Below Average
☆	Lowest

Source: Morningstar, Inc.

Morningstar, Inc. Morningstar uses a star method for rating purposes. The risk-adjusted rating combines both performance and risk together to determine one evaluation. The fund's Morningstar Risk-Adjusted Rating is calculated by subtracting the fund's Morningstar Risk score from the fund's Morningstar Return score. The resulting number is plotted along a curve to determine the fund's rating for each time period. If the fund scores in the top 10 percent of its broad investment category, it receives five stars (highest). If the fund scores in the next 22.5 percent, it receives four stars (above average). Similarly, if the fund scores in the middle 35 percent, it receives three stars (neutral or average). The funds that fall in the next 22.5 percent receive two stars (below average). Finally, the funds that fall in the bottom 10 percent, receive one star (lowest). The star rating may be for a given period such as three, five, or ten years. Therefore, the Morningstar's rating system ranks funds relative to other funds and not necessarily on an absolute basis. Figure 16.4 shows Morningstar's mutual fund ratings.

Standard & Poor's. A Standard & Poor's mutual bond fund credit quality rating is an assessment of the overall credit quality of a fund's investments and level of protection a portfolio provides against principal losses from credit defaults. The assessment is based on a review of a fund's portfolio assets, eligible investments, and counterparties. A mutual bond fund credit rating is not a recommendation to purchase, sell, or hold a security, inasmuch as it does not comment as to market price, yield, or suitability for a particular investor. The assessment does not take

Figure 16.5   Standard & Poor's Mutual Bond Fund Ratings

Rating	Description
AAAf	The fund's portfolio holdings and counterparties provide extremely strong protection against losses from credit defaults.
AAf	The fund's portfolio holdings and counterparties provide very strong protection against losses from credit defaults.
Af	The fund's portfolio holdings and counterparties provide strong protection against losses from credit defaults.
BBBf	The fund's portfolio holdings and counterparties provide adequate protection against losses from credit defaults.
BBf	The fund's portfolio holdings and/or counterparties provide uncertain protection against losses from credit defaults.
Bf	The fund's portfolio holdings and/or counterparties exhibit vulnerability to losses from credit defaults.
CCCf	The fund's portfolio holdings and/or counterparties make it extremely vulnerable to losses from credit defaults.

Ratings from "AAf" to "CCCf" may be modified by the addition of a plus (+) or minus (–) sign to relative standing within the major rating categories.

Source: Reprinted by permission by Standard & Poor's, a division of The McGraw-Hill Companies.

into account the extent to which fund activities, including the allocation of expenses, the possible sale of investments prior to their maturity at a loss, and/or hedging operations, might affect the yield to investors, or the extent to which interest rate fluctuations might affect the market prices of the fund's shares. Figure 16.5 shows Standard & Poor's Mutual Bond Fund Credit Quality Ratings.

Value Line. Value Line ranks mutual funds with an overall ranking for performance and a ranking for risk. Funds are ranked in three separate broad groups: equity, fixed income, and municipal bond. Figure 16.6 shows the Value Line mutual fund ranking categories.

Figure 16.6   Value Line Mutual Fund Ranking Categories

Overall Rank		Risk Rank	
1	Highest	1	Lowest Risk
2	Above Average	2	Lower Risk
3	Average	3	Average Risk
4	Below Average	4	Higher Risk
5	Lowest	5	Highest Risk

Source: *Value Line Mutual Fund Survey,* New York, N.Y.

Analyzing Stocks and Bonds

Two schools of analyzing stock and bond prices are Traditional Portfolio Theory (TPT) and Modern Portfolio Theory (MPT). Both theories analyze and quantify mutual funds. However, before a mutual fund can be analyzed, the fund's portfolio of underlying securities must be analyzed and quantified. Quality of the underlying securities is an important factor when using either TPT or MPT.

Traditional Portfolio Theory

Traditional Portfolio Theory utilizes technical analysis, fundamental analysis, or a combination of both when researching a company, an industry, or the overall market. Bonds are primarily analyzed by maturity, credit rating, debt service coverage, level of interest rates, current and expected economic growth, and how they are impacted by Federal Reserve Board policies.

Technical analysis. *Technical analysis* uses stock price movements and trading volumes to determine if the stock's price is overvalued or undervalued. The technical analyst, also known as a *technician* or *chartist,* uses previous trading ranges, chart patterns, trendlines, and other price and volume ratios for research. The terms *overbought* and *oversold* are sometimes used interchangeably with overvalued and undervalued, respectively.

Fundamental analysis. *Fundamental analysis* uses financial ratios, quality of company's management, product market share, and economic factors to determine if the stock's current price is overvalued or undervalued. A particular group of stocks, an industry, or the overall market can be analyzed by fundamental analysis. Some of the basic financial ratios that analysts and investors employ are earnings per share (EPS), price-earnings (PE) ratio, price–cash flow ratio, book value per share, dividends per share, dividend payout ratio, and dividend yield.

Earnings per share. Earnings per share is one of the most important financial statistics used by investors and research analysts. *Earnings per share* is calculated by dividing a company's net profit by the total amount of common stock shares outstanding. Simply stated, *net profit* is calculated by subtracting from net sales (revenues) all operating costs, interest expense, preferred stock dividends, and taxes.

Analysts and investors look for increased EPS growth for three reasons:

1. Increased EPS may mean a higher stock price based on PE ratios.
2. There is a possibility of a dividend payment or increased dividend payment.
3. There is sufficient cash flow to expand business operations, thus increasing EPS and dividends in the future.

I/B/E/S International Inc. supplies the I/B/E/S database, which maintains the largest historical database of consensus and individual analyst data and provides analysts' estimates of future earnings for thousands of publicly-traded companies. I/B/E/S represents the Institutional Brokers Estimates System. Earnings-per-share estimates from securities analysts are tabulated showing the high, low, and average (consensus) estimates. Actual EPS reported by the company are compared to the consensus EPS to determine if the earnings reported are in line with the estimates or if an earnings "surprise" occurred. An earnings *surprise* means that the level of earnings reported was higher or lower than the market expected. A favorable surprise (earnings higher than expected) may cause the stock price to increase. An unfavorable surprise (earnings lower than expected) may cause the stock price to decline. The magnitude of the difference between the EPS and the estimated EPS may cause the stock price to rise or fall proportionately. Major EPS surprises for some of the most well-known companies may cause the market as a whole to rise or fall, at least temporarily. The I/B/E/S reports also detail how many estimates are available on each company, along with other pertinent financial information.

Price-earnings ratio. Price-earnings ratio measures what the market is paying for the earnings per share of the company. The *price-earnings ratio* (also known as the *multiple*) is computed by dividing the current market price of a stock by the reported latest 12 months' EPS. The PE ratio also may be computed using the next year's forecasted EPS. Typically, newspapers report PE ratios using the trailing 12 months' earnings per share.

The usefulness of the ratio is to compare the stock's current PE ratio to the stock's historical PE ratios. If the PE ratio is relatively low, this may indicate that the stock's price is undervalued (possibly a good time to buy). Likewise, if the PE ratio is relatively high, this may indicate that the stock's price is overvalued (possibly a good time to sell). Comparisons also can be made to the industry's average PE multiple or to a corresponding market index PE multiple.

A high PE ratio also may indicate that the marketplace is forecasting significantly higher earnings growth for the coming year. A low PE ratio may indicate that the marketplace is forecasting lower earnings growth for the coming year. Generally, companies with low PE ratios have higher dividend yields than companies with higher PE ratios. Of course, the PE ratio is only one factor in determining the type of stock (value or growth), the valuation of the stock, and whether the stock should be purchased or sold.

The price-earnings ratio for a mutual fund is typically the weighted average of the PE ratios for the fund's underlying stocks. Mutual funds whose investment objective is long-term growth or growth and income generally own stocks with relatively low PE ratios, which are also known as *value stocks.* Mutual funds whose investment objective is aggressive growth or capital appreciation generally own stocks with relatively high PE ratios, which are also known as *growth stocks.*

Book value per share. Book value of a company is computed by subtracting total liabilities from total assets. *Book value per share* is calculated by dividing the book value (also known as *net worth*) by the total outstanding common stock shares.

Price-book ratio. Price-book (PB) ratio measures what the market is paying for the book value per share of the company. The price-book ratio is computed by dividing the current market price of a stock by the current book value per share.

The usefulness of the ratio is to compare the stock's current PB ratio to the stock's historical PB ratios. If the PB ratio is relatively low, this may indicate that the stock's price is undervalued. Likewise, if the PB ratio is relatively high, this may indicate that the stock's price is overvalued. Comparisons also can be made to the industry's average PB multiple or to a corresponding market index PB multiple.

A low PB ratio may indicate that the stock is undervalued based on the liquidation value of the company's assets. Also, a stock with a low PB ratio may be a candidate for a buyout or merger that could cause the stock price to appreciate significantly. Generally, companies with low PB ratios have higher dividend yields than companies with higher PB ratios. Of course, the PB ratio is only one factor in determining the type of stock (value or growth), the valuation of the stock, and whether the stock should be purchased or sold.

The price-book ratio for a mutual fund is typically the weighted average of the PB ratios for the fund's underlying stocks. Mutual funds whose investment objective is long-term growth or growth and income generally own stocks with relatively low PB ratios (also known as *value stocks*). Mutual funds whose investment objective is aggressive growth or capital appreciation generally own stocks with relatively high PB ratios (also known as *growth stocks*).

Price–cash flow ratio. Price–cash flow (PC) ratio measures what the market is paying for the cash per share of the company. The *price–cash flow ratio* is computed by dividing the current market price of a stock by the reported latest 12 months' cash flow per share. The PC ratio also may be computed using the next year's forecasted cash flow per share.

The usefulness of the ratio is to compare the stock's current PC ratio to the stock's historical PC ratios. If the PC ratio is relatively low, this may indicate that the stock's price is undervalued (possibly a good time to buy). Likewise, if the PC ratio is relatively high, then this may indicate that the stock's price is overvalued (possibly a good time to sell). Comparisons also can be made to the industry's average PC multiple or to a corresponding market index PC multiple.

A high PC ratio also may indicate that the marketplace is forecasting significantly higher cash flow for the coming year. A low PC ratio may indicate that the marketplace is forecasting lower cash flow for the coming year. Cash flow figures measure the company's ability to generate cash, meet current obligations, and pay dividends. Of course, the PC ratio is only one factor in determining the type of stock (value or growth), the valuation of the stock, and whether the stock should be purchased or sold.

The price–cash flow ratio for a mutual fund is typically the weighted average of the PC ratios for the fund's underlying stocks. Mutual funds whose investment objective is long-term growth or growth and income generally own stocks with relatively low PC ratios, which also are known as *value stocks.* Mutual funds whose investment objective is aggressive growth or capital appreciation generally own stocks with relatively high PC ratios, which also are known as *growth stocks.*

Cash flow analysis and price–cash flow ratios are normally used when analyzing international companies. Accounting methods, such as calculating EPS, and financial disclosure are not always uniform to the United States accounting practices. Therefore, cash flow analysis may be a better indicator for an international company's profitability than the earnings per share. Thus, portfolio managers for international mutual funds may use cash flow analysis as one indicator when purchasing international stocks.

Dividend per share. Dividend per share is the cash amount paid by the company to its common shareholders. Dividends are declared by the board of directors and typically paid quarterly. In some cases, the company may pay the dividend in the form of additional shares rather than cash, which is known as a *stock dividend.* Investors and analysts look for a company to increase its dividend, which usually is a sign of continued profitability.

Dividend payout ratio. Dividend payout ratio is the percent of earnings per share paid to the common shareholder in the form of a cash dividend. The dividend payout ratio is calculated by dividing the dividend per share by the earnings per share and multiplying by 100.

A low dividend payout ratio generally means the company is reinvesting a substantial portion of the earnings in its own operations for expansion and research and development. The company uses its own earnings for expansion to provide a greater growth of earnings per share rather than paying dividends to shareholders. Hopefully, a higher earnings growth benefits shareholders by producing a higher stock price. Growth companies typically have low dividend payout ratios.

A high dividend payout ratio generally means the company is a more mature company whose earnings growth is not increasing rapidly each year. The company pays out a substantially high percent of its earnings to shareholders to reward shareholders and hopefully increase the stock price with higher dividend payments. Companies whose stock is categorized as a value stock often have high dividend payout ratios. However, a high dividend payout ratio also may be a negative sign if the earnings per share decreases substantially, causing the dividend payout ratio to increase. Furthermore, if sufficient earnings are not generated to pay the dividend, the dividend may be reduced or eliminated.

Dividend yield. The dividend yield measures the income return that a shareholder receives from owning a company's stock. The *yield* is quoted as an annualized percent. The *dividend yield* is calculated by dividing the current annual dividend per share by the current market price per share of the stock. A relatively high dividend yield may indicate that the stock is considered an *income stock* or value stock. A low dividend yield may indicate that the stock is considered a growth stock. Of course, the dividend yield is only one factor in determining the type of stock (value or growth), the valuation of the stock, and whether the stock should be purchased or sold.

Mutual funds whose investment objective is long-term growth or growth and income usually own stocks with relatively high dividend yields. Mutual funds whose investment objective is aggressive growth or capital appreciation generally own stocks with relatively low or no dividend yields.

Maturity. A bond's maturity length usually determines the volatility (price change) of a bond or note when interest rates change. When interest rates increase, prices of bonds and bond funds decrease. When interest rates decrease, prices of bonds and bond funds increase. The longer the bond or note's maturity, the more volatile the price is when interest rates change. If interest rates are rising, prices of shorter maturities decline less than prices of longer maturities. If interest rates are falling, prices of shorter maturities increase less than prices of longer maturities.

Average maturity of a bond fund's portfolio is the weighted average of all of the maturities of the fund's underlying bonds. The average maturity may or may not be close to the duration of the bond portfolio, depending on such factors as the type of bonds, call features, maturity dates, coupon rates, and payment dates. Generally, however, the longer the average maturity of a fund's portfolio, the more volatile the fund's price (NAV) is when interest rates change. The shorter the average maturity of a fund's portfolio, the less volatile the fund's price (NAV) is when interest rates change.

Average maturity of a bond mutual fund's portfolio is important because it shows you the potential volatility of the fund when interest rates change. A comparison of one fund's average maturity to another fund's average maturity gives you some insight into the risks associated between the two bond funds. Additionally, if interest rates are relatively high you may want to purchase a bond fund with a longer average maturity. Conversely, if interest rates are relatively low, you may want to purchase a bond fund with a shorter average maturity.

Debt service. Debt service is the cash required by the issuer of a note or bond to pay all interest and principal payments that usually are due within one year.

Debt service coverage. Debt service coverage is expressed as a ratio showing how much cash is available to pay all interest and principal payments that usually are due within one year. The higher the ratio, the higher the issuer's ability to pay the interest and principal when due.

Federal Reserve Board Policies

One of the chief responsibilities of the Federal Reserve Board (also known as the *Fed*) is to control inflation. The Board attempts to control inflation by changing interest rates and money supply. Generally, lowering interest rates and increasing the money supply help the economy to expand. Increasing interest rates and reducing the money supply help the economy to contract. In theory, raising interest rates usually reduces inflation and lowering interest rates usually increases inflation. The Fed tries to control interest rates and money supply by buying and selling government securities in the marketplace. When the Fed sells securities in the marketplace, they are attempting to reduce the money supply and raise interest rates. When the Fed buys securities in the marketplace, they are attempting to increase the money supply and lower interest rates.

The Fed also changes the discount rate to attempt to control interest rates and inflation. The *discount rate* is the interest rate the Fed charges to its member banks when they borrow from the Fed. Most banks set their interest rates for loans based on the discount rate or other prevailing short-term interest rates. The *prime rate* is typically the best interest rate that the biggest banks charge their best customers. The *federal funds* rate is the interest rate that one bank charges another bank for borrowing money, usually overnight. The federal funds rate is set daily by the marketplace and provides a good indicator of interest rate movements.

Modern Portfolio Theory

Many academic and investment research analysts use Modern Portfolio Theory (MPT) when analyzing mutual funds. *MPT* concentrates on the risk and return associated with individual mutual funds, a group of mutual funds, and/or a corresponding market index. MPT tries to quantify the relationship between risk and return. Some of the components used are:

- Correlation coefficient (R)
- Coefficient of determination (R-squared)
- Beta
- Alpha
- Excess return
- Standard deviation
- Sharpe ratio
- Duration

Correlation coefficient (R). Correlation coefficient (R) is the statistical measurement showing the relationship between the movements of two variables, such as comparing the price change of one mutual fund to the price change of a particular market index. Correlation coefficient has a range of –1.00 and 1.00. A correlation coefficient of 1 means that the mutual fund's price movement is completely (100 percent) related to the movement of the corresponding market index. A correlation coefficient of .4 means that the mutual fund's price movement is only 40 percent related to the movement of the corresponding market index.

If the correlation coefficient is negative, then the mutual fund's price movement is opposite of the movement of the corresponding market index.

Coefficient of determination (R-squared). The coefficient of determination (R-squared) is a positive number ranging from 0 to 1. (Some research analysts, however, show the range of R-squared from 0 to 100.) The R-squared is the correlation coefficient times itself, or squared. R-squared signifies the reliability of the beta and alpha coefficients. The higher the R-squared, the more reliable are the beta and alpha coefficients. The lower the R-squared, the less reliable are the beta and alpha coefficients.

Beta coefficient. Beta coefficient (also known as beta) measures the volatility of a mutual fund's price movement as compared to the price movement of a respective market. Any market may be used as a benchmark market, depending on the mutual fund being analyzed and measured. The market being used for comparison purposes is given a beta coefficient of 1.00. If a mutual fund has a beta coefficient higher than 1.00, then the mutual fund is more volatile than the market. Conversely, if the mutual fund has a beta coefficient lower than 1.00, the mutual fund is less volatile than the market. For example, if a mutual fund has a beta of 1.2 and the market increases by 10 percent, then the mutual fund's price should increase by 12 percent (1.2 × 10 percent). Likewise, if the beta is .8 and the market increases by 10 percent, then the mutual fund's price should rise by 8 percent (.8 × 10 percent).

Conversely, if a mutual fund has a beta of 1.3 and the market decreases by 10 percent, then the mutual fund's price should decrease by

13 percent (1.3 × 10 percent). Likewise, if the beta is .7 and the market decreases by 10 percent, then the mutual fund's price should decrease by 7 percent (.7 × 10 percent).

Conservative investors who want less volatility (less return but less risk) may want to concentrate on mutual funds with lower beta coefficients. More aggressive investors who want higher returns and are willing to accept higher risks may want to concentrate on funds with higher beta coefficients.

Alpha coefficient. Alpha coefficient measures the difference between the return the mutual fund actually earns and the expected return based on the fund's beta coefficient. Thus, a positive alpha number shows that the fund performed better than expected based on the fund's beta. A negative alpha number shows that the fund performed worse than expected based on the fund's beta.

Alpha numbers are used sometimes to determine the portfolio manager's added value to the performance of the mutual fund. A positive number means that the manager added value to the fund; its performance was better than the expected performance based on the market's performance and the fund's beta. A negative number means that the manager subtracted value from the fund; its performance was worse than the expected performance based on the market's performance and the fund's beta.

Excess return. Excess return is the amount of return for a given period of time in excess of the return from a risk-free investment for the same period of time. A risk-free investment is considered a 90-day U.S. Treasury bill, if held to maturity, or a federally insured certificate of deposit.

Standard deviation. Standard deviation is a measure of variation between the mutual fund's return and the mean (average) return. Standard deviation represents the volatility of the fund's returns. Therefore, the standard deviation signifies the risk associated with the mutual fund's performance. The higher the standard deviation, the higher the expected risk associated with the fund's price movement. The lower the standard deviation, the lower the expected risk associated with the fund's price movement.

Many investors expect higher returns when assuming higher risks. A higher standard deviation may indicate higher expected returns and a lower standard deviation may indicate lower expected returns.

Sharpe ratio. The Sharpe ratio is used to show the fund's historical risk-adjusted performance. To compute the Sharpe ratio, the annualized excess return is divided by the standard deviation of the fund's annualized excess returns. The higher the number, the better the fund's historical risk-adjusted performance.

Duration. Duration measures a bond's volatility based on changes of interest rates. Duration is a weighted-average term-to-maturity of the bond's cash flows, the weights being the present value of each cash flow as a percentage of the bond's full price. The greater the duration of a bond, the greater its percentage volatility. In general, duration rises with maturity, falls with frequency of coupon payments, and falls as the yield rises (the higher yield reduces the present values of the cash flows). For working purposes, duration can be defined as the approximate percentage change in price for a 100 basis point (1 percent) change in yield. For example, duration means the price of the bond will change by approximately 5 percent for a 100 basis point change in yield. (Source: *Barron's Finance & Investment Handbook.*)

Duration of a bond mutual fund is important because it shows you the potential volatility of the fund when interest rates change. A comparison of one fund's duration to another fund's duration gives you some insight into the comparative risks of two bond funds. If interest rates are relatively high, you may want to purchase a bond fund with a longer duration. Likewise, if interest rates are relatively low, you may want to purchase a bond fund with a shorter duration.

CHAPTER 17

Managing Your Mutual Fund Portfolio

The first and most important aspect in managing your portfolio is asset allocation. The decision of what percentages you want in money market funds, bond funds, and stock funds is paramount to portfolio management. Because portfolio management is not a defined art, many different allocations may be appropriate for you.

Typical Portfolios

A typical portfolio asset allocation model includes all three asset categories. Figure 17.1 shows a portfolio asset allocation model assuming a primary investment objective of capital appreciation and a secondary objective of income.

FIGURE 17.1   Sample Portfolio Asset Allocation Model for Capital Appreciation and Income

Money Market Mutual Funds	10%
Bond Mutual Funds	30%
Stock Mutual Funds	60%

A beneficial starting point is to adjust the sample portfolio asset allocation model for a typical person to a specific asset allocation for you based on your investor's profile (see Chapter 10). The following individual profiles show how the portfolio model could be adjusted to reflect your own personal asset allocation. (The revised portfolios are only for illustration purposes and may need to be further adjusted based on your personal investment profile.)

Retired person. A retired person usually prefers investments that offer a steady income with stability of principal. However, because many people are living longer than ever expected, some retired people may need to continue investing in some growth mutual funds in order to maintain their accustomed lifestyle and to keep pace with inflation.

Therefore, you may want to adjust the portfolio asset allocation for a typical person by increasing the percent in the money market fund portion, increasing the percent in the bond mutual fund portion, and decreasing the percent in the stock mutual fund portion.

Figure 17.2 shows the revised portfolio asset allocation for a retired person over 75 years of age.

FIGURE 17.2   Revised Sample Portfolio Asset Allocation for a Retired Person over 75 Years of Age

Money Market Mutual Funds	15%
Bond Mutual Funds	65%
Stock Mutual Funds	20%

FIGURE 17.3   Revised Sample Portfolio Asset Allocation for a Retired Person over 65 Years of Age

Money Market Mutual Funds	15%
Bond Mutual Funds	50%
Stock Mutual Funds	35%

Figure 17.3 shows the revised portfolio asset allocation for a retired person over 65 years of age.

Middle-aged person. A middle-aged person may want a combination of income-oriented and growth-oriented investments to supplement his or her salary, as well as build assets for a second home, travel, or retirement.

Therefore, you may want to adjust the portfolio asset allocation for a typical person by decreasing the percent in the bond mutual fund portion and increasing the percent in the stock mutual fund portion.

Figure 17.4 shows the portfolio asset allocation revised for a middle-aged person.

Young person. A young person may want a growth-oriented investment in order to accumulate more assets for a first home, travel, education, or early retirement.

Therefore, you may want to adjust the portfolio asset allocation for a typical person by decreasing the percent in the bond mutual fund portion and increasing the percent in the stock mutual fund portion.

Figure 17.5 shows the revised portfolio asset allocation for a young person.

FIGURE 17.4   Revised Sample Portfolio Asset Allocation for a Middle-Aged Person

Money Market Mutual Funds	10%
Bond Mutual Funds	25%
Stock Mutual Funds	65%

FIGURE 17.5 Revised Sample Portfolio Asset Allocation for a Young Person

Money Market Mutual Funds	10%
Bond Mutual Funds	15%
Stock Mutual Funds	75%

Child. Parents, grandparents, and other family members may invest for a child's education and future benefit. An income-oriented investment or a growth-oriented investment may be used depending on the market outlook and risk aversion. The child's age is a major factor in deciding how to invest the money. Typically, the younger the child, the more growth-oriented the investment may be. If the child is nearing the age where he or she may need the money for college or another purpose, the mutual fund investment may be changed to a more conservative, stable investment, such as a money market fund.

Therefore, you may want to adjust the portfolio asset allocation for a typical person by decreasing the percent in the bond mutual fund portion and increasing the percent in the stock mutual fund portion.

Figure 17.6 shows the revised portfolio asset allocation for a child 12 years of age or under.

If the child is over 12 years old and needs the money for college or another purpose, then begin decreasing the stock mutual fund portion and increasing the money market fund portion as he or she gets closer to needing the money. If, however, the child is over 12 years old and doesn't need the money for college, but rather for a house or another purpose when he or she is 21 years old or older, then it still may be appropriate to leave a large portion in the stock mutual fund category.

FIGURE 17.6 Revised Sample Portfolio Asset Allocation for a Child 12 Years of Age or Under

Money Market Mutual Funds	10%
Bond Mutual Funds	10%
Stock Mutual Funds	80%

FIGURE 17.7 Revised Sample Portfolio Asset Allocation for a High Tax-bracket Person

Money Market Mutual Funds	5%
Bond Mutual Funds	20%
Stock Mutual Funds	75%

High tax-bracket person. A high tax-bracket person may want tax-free or tax-deferred income investments. Also, individuals who are in a high tax bracket may prefer capital growth instead of income. Capital gains are only taxed when realized and, therefore, the taxes are deferred until he or she sells the mutual fund or when the fund pays a capital gain distribution. The capital gains tax rate also may be lower than the tax rate for income.

Therefore, you may want to adjust the portfolio asset allocation for a typical person by decreasing the percent in the money market fund portion, decreasing the percent in the bond mutual fund portion, and increasing the percent in the stock mutual fund portion.

Figure 17.7 shows the revised portfolio asset allocation for a high tax-bracket person.

Individual investor's profiles are infinite and, therefore, there could be numerous portfolio asset allocations. As your age, financial condition, investment objectives, goals, and risk tolerance change over time, you should adjust your asset allocation so your investment portfolio is positioned to achieve your new objectives and goals.

Diversification

After allocating your assets, decide how to diversify each category. Purchasing mutual funds makes part of the diversification process easier. When you invest in a mutual fund, the fund provides you with diversification of individual securities immediately. However, most mutual funds own similar types of securities. Therefore, the next step for diversifying your portfolio is to determine the types of mutual funds you want to purchase. You must decide how many funds you want to own in each category. Also, how many funds in total do you want to own?

Types of Money Market Funds

Typically, you only need one money market fund. Do you want the income from the money market fund to be taxable or tax-exempt? If you are in a high tax bracket (28 percent or higher), then a tax-free money market fund is probably more suitable. However, you also need to calculate the return from a tax-exempt money market fund versus the after-tax return from a taxable money market fund. Determine which gives you the highest after-tax return and select the fund.

If you are very conservative, you may want a money market fund comprised of only government securities or an insured money market account.

Types of Bond Mutual Funds

If you are purchasing a bond fund, you have many considerations. The first two considerations are the fund's average length of maturity and the duration of the portfolio of underlying bonds. Because most bond mutual funds do not have a maturity date, you *cannot* expect to receive your principal on a certain date. Furthermore, as interest rates increase, the net asset value (NAV) of the bond mutual fund decreases; as interest rates decrease, the NAV of the bond mutual fund increases. The longer the average length of maturity or duration of the fund's portfolio of underlying bonds, the more volatile the fund's NAV is when interest rates change. Thus, when you are considering purchasing a bond mutual fund, it is better to buy one when interest rates are higher than when they are lower. However, it is extremely difficult to predict interest rate movements. You might want to follow these guidelines: If interest rates are considered to be on a lower level than a higher level, you may want to invest in a short-term or intermediate-term bond fund. If interest rates are considered to be on a higher level than a lower level, you may want to invest in a long-term bond fund.

However, a target maturity fund does have a maturity date (i.e., the date the fund intends to liquidate the fund's assets and return the principal to the shareholder). Of course, there is no guarantee that the fund will be able to achieve its investment objective.

The next consideration is credit ratings or quality of the portfolio of bonds. Bond funds can be categorized by the quality (credit rating) of the underlying bonds. Bonds funds may hold bonds rated only high grade, medium grade, or low grade, or in some cases all three categories. Normally, the higher the quality of bonds, the lower the fund's distribution rate. Furthermore, the lower the quality of bonds, the higher is the potential risk of loss of principal due to defaults of the underlying bonds. Based on your investor's profile, especially your risk tolerance, you can decide whether a lower-yielding, higher-quality bond mutual fund or a higher-yielding, lower-quality bond mutual fund is suitable for you. Also, the dividend income paid by bonds may vary based on the interest earned from the fund's portfolio of underlying bonds after the fund's operating expenses.

Another consideration is the income tax status of the mutual fund. If you are in a high tax bracket (28 percent or higher), then a tax-free bond mutual fund is probably more suitable. Prior to investing in a bond fund, calculate the return on the income from investing in a tax-exempt bond mutual fund versus the after-tax return on the income from a taxable bond mutual fund. Determine which gives you the highest *after-tax* return and select that type of fund. The fund's distribution rate is appropriate to use for determining the current income return from the bond fund for this type of comparison. When making a comparison, you should use similar bond mutual funds that have underlying bonds of comparable quality (credit rating) and length of maturity. For example, a tax-exempt municipal bond fund with underlying long-term investment-grade bonds could be compared to a taxable corporate bond fund with underlying long-term investment-grade bonds. Another example for comparison purposes is a tax-exempt bond fund with underlying long-term, insured municipal bonds and a taxable bond fund with underlying long-term government bonds.

Tax-exempt bond fund. Assuming you select a tax-exempt bond fund based on your tax bracket and the difference between the distribution rates, you then need to decide the type of tax-exempt bond mutual fund.

Your first decision is whether you want a national tax-exempt bond fund or a tax-exempt bond fund that holds bonds issued by your state of residence. Of course, if your state has no income tax, intangible tax, or tangible tax, etc., you do not have to consider this aspect. In all probability, if your state has no tax liability, a mutual fund for your state does not exist.

If a mutual fund for your state does exist, then you need to compare the after-tax return (including state taxes) on the income from a national tax-exempt bond fund and the after-tax return on the income from your state's tax-exempt bond fund—and be sure the underlying bonds are of comparable quality (credit rating) and average length of maturity.

Taxable bond fund. Assuming you select a taxable bond fund based on your tax bracket and the difference between the distribution rates, you then need to decide the type of taxable bond mutual fund.

Your first decision is whether you want a domestic or international bond mutual fund. If you are beginning to invest, you should concentrate on purchasing a domestic bond mutual fund. If you are a more experienced investor or have adequate financial assets, then you may want to consider purchasing an international bond fund. In either case, the portion that you invest in international bond mutual funds should normally be less relative to the portion in domestic bond mutual funds.

Domestic taxable bond mutual funds. Domestic taxable bond mutual funds include corporate and government bond funds. Typically, corporate bond funds offer higher yields than government bond funds that have underlying bonds with comparable lengths of maturities. If higher yielding bond funds with lower quality underlying bonds are suitable for you then you should consider corporate bond funds.

Taxable corporate bond funds. Generally, corporate bond funds can be categorized by the quality (credit rating) of the underlying bonds as investment grade or below investment grade. Bonds rated investment grade are rated in the four highest ratings by Standard & Poor's and by Moody's. Some funds only purchase A-rated or better bonds for the portfolio.

Bonds rated below the four highest ratings are known as junk bonds. Bond funds that purchase bonds rated below investment grade are called junk bond or high-yield funds. Based on your investor's profile, especially your risk tolerance, you can decide whether a lower-yielding, high-quality bond mutual fund or a higher-yielding, lower-quality bond mutual fund is suitable for you.

Some funds purchase convertible bonds, which are convertible into common stock. A convertible bond pays interest to its bondholders, and the bond price rises and falls primarily based on the movement of the common stock price according to the terms of the conversion and changes in interest rates. Convertible bonds are sometimes referred to as equity-related securities, because they may be converted into common stock (equity). Thus, convertible bond funds usually do not pay as much income and may be more volatile than bond funds that own only nonconvertible bonds.

Taxable government bond funds. Government bond funds primarily hold U.S. Treasury securities and federal government agency securities although some funds only hold one or the other. U.S. Treasury securities and some federal agency securities are guaranteed by the U.S. government for the repayment of principal and interest when due. However, the government bond mutual funds that hold U.S. Treasury and federal agency securities are not guaranteed by the U.S. government for the payment of principal or interest income. Government bond mutual funds share prices fluctuate with changes in interest rates. If lower-yielding government bond funds with the highest quality of underlying bonds (as compared to corporate bond funds) are suitable for you, then you should consider government bond funds.

Taxable index bond funds. Index bond funds may be used to target a particular market segment. Index funds offer diversification, low costs, and generally competitive performance based on the index used.

Taxable international bond mutual funds. International bond mutual funds may include bonds issued by foreign corporations and foreign governments. International bond mutual funds offer income returns that may not correlate with the returns from domestic bond mutual funds. International interest rates may differ from domestic interest rates. Therefore, prices of international bond funds may rise and fall contrary to the prices of domestic bond funds. Furthermore, international bond funds carry currency risk. International bond funds may be a good method of diversifying the bond portion of your portfolio only if you understand the differences between domestic bond funds and international bond funds. International index bond funds may be used to target a particular market segment.

Types of Stock Mutual Funds

Your first decision is whether you want a domestic or international stock mutual fund. If you want to diversify, buying both domestic and international stock funds helps to accomplish this. If you are beginning to invest, you should consider concentrating on purchasing domestic stock mutual funds for the stock portion of your portfolio. If you are a more experienced investor or have higher risk tolerance, then you may want to consider purchasing international stock funds. In either case, the portion that you invest in international stock mutual funds should normally be less relative to the portion in domestic stock mutual funds.

Domestic stock mutual funds. The variety and types of domestic stock mutual funds are so numerous that it is difficult to list all of the different types. At least a few basic stock funds should be purchased for the stock mutual fund portion of your portfolio. The six primary stock funds that you may want to initially consider are:

1. Aggressive growth funds
2. Growth funds
3. Growth and income funds
4. Index funds
5. Utility funds
6. One or two sector funds

If your portfolio is sizable and you want additional diversification, you may want to add other types of domestic stock mutual funds to your portfolio.

Sector funds. Sector funds allow you to invest in one particular industry and sometimes in two or more industries. Because the particular industry may be more volatile than the overall market, you have more risk than in a broadly diversified stock fund. However, you may achieve a higher return if the industry does better than the general market. Sector funds allow you to invest in a market segment that may have higher growth rates than other segments. One or two sector funds may be suitable for your stock mutual fund portion depending on your investor's profile and other stock funds you are holding. Structuring your portfolio with several different types of sector funds may provide additional diversification.

International stock mutual funds. The variety and types of international stock mutual funds are so numerous that it is difficult to list all of the different types. At least a few basic international stock funds should be purchased for the stock mutual fund portion of your portfolio. The five primary stock funds that you may want to initially consider are:

1. Large-cap growth funds
2. Small-cap and mid-cap growth funds
3. Index funds
4. Utility funds
5. One, two, or three single country or region funds

If your portfolio is sizable and you want additional diversification, then you may want to add other types of international stock mutual funds to your portfolio. Besides the regular market risk associated with stock mutual funds, international stock funds also carry currency risk.

Composition of Your Portfolio

Now that asset allocation, diversification, and types of mutual funds have been discussed, the process of selecting individual mutual funds begins. You need to determine your asset allocation for each category:

1. Money market funds
2. Bond funds
3. Stock funds

Typically, most people usually own either an income-oriented portfolio or a growth-oriented portfolio. Obviously, some people own a portfolio that is both income-oriented and growth-oriented.

You need to determine the *percent* you want to invest in each asset category (money market funds, bonds funds, and stock funds), and the *number* of funds you want to own in each category.

✐ Your Investor's Guide

Your Portfolio Asset Allocation

Money Market Mutual Funds _____ %

Bond Mutual Funds _____ %

Stock Mutual Funds _____ %

Your Investor's Guide allows you to complete your asset allocation based on your investment policy statement.

Depending on your financial resources and available assets, the number of funds you own initially or over time will vary. From a portfolio management point of view, ten to 13 mutual funds (excluding money market funds) may be a desirable number of mutual funds to own. Depending on your financial situation and investment objective, ten to 13 mutual funds should offer you adequate diversification across many types of market segments, geographical regions, and types of securities. Many academic studies are used to determine the number of funds needed to achieve optimum portfolio diversification and asset allocation. However, the combination of types of funds is so high that it is virtually impossible to decide on an exact number of funds to own that will provide the optimum portfolio diversification and asset allocation for mutual funds.

Ten to 13 mutual funds (excluding money market funds) should be manageable from a recordkeeping and monitoring point of view. It is more difficult to monitor and maintain proper accounting records for 20 to 30 different mutual funds than for ten to 13 funds.

Your first step in achieving your investment objectives and goals is to establish a diversified portfolio of funds. Assuming you decide to use only one fund family, you need to know basically all of the types of funds available to you in the family. If you decide to use two fund families, then you need to know basically all of the funds in both families. By knowing all of the funds available you can develop a portfolio of mutual funds based on your current financial situation with the outlook to purchase other funds as you add more money to your portfolio.

FIGURE 17.8 Sample Portfolio Asset Allocation for a Retired Person over 75 Years of Age

Money Market Mutual Funds	15%
Bond Mutual Funds	65%
Stock Mutual Funds	20%

Once you understand your choices, your next step is decide which individual mutual funds are suitable for your portfolio. Your investment professional can assist you in selecting the appropriate fund family, individual funds, and asset allocation.

Income-Oriented Portfolio

If you are income-oriented, you normally need to be invested in more money market funds and bond funds than stock funds. Therefore, you may want to have one money market fund, several bond funds, and some stock funds. Even though you may nearly have as many stock funds as money market funds and bond funds, the percent invested in the stock fund portion is less than in the money market fund and bond fund portion combined. Typically, you do not need as many bond funds as stock funds to be adequately diversified.

For example, if you fall in the category of a retired person over the age of 75 years, see Figure 17.8 for a sample asset allocation.

Figure 17.9 shows the number and type of mutual funds for a portfolio for a person over 75 years of age.

The percent invested in each of the individual funds is dependent on your investor's profile, investment objective, and risk tolerance. Some funds listed in the example may not be suitable for you. Dividends and capital gains distributions should be paid in cash if you need the income. Otherwise, have them reinvested in more shares of the mutual fund or in another fund in the family.

If you fall in the category of a retired person over the age of 65, your asset allocation may be the following as shown in Figure 17.10.

Figure 17.11 shows the number and type of mutual funds for a portfolio for a person over 65 years of age.

FIGURE 17.9   Sample Portfolio for a Person over 75 Years of Age

Money Market Mutual Funds:
   1 Money market fund

Bond Mutual Funds:
   1 Long-term government bond fund
   1 Intermediate-term government bond fund
   1 Short-term government bond fund
   1 Long-term corporate bond fund (investment grade)
   1 Intermediate-term corporate bond fund (investment grade)
   1 International bond fund–government and corporate
      (investment grade)

Stock Mutual Funds:
   1 Growth fund
   1 Growth and income stock fund
   1 Utility stock fund
   1 International stock fund–region

The percent invested in each of the individual funds is dependent on your investor's profile, investment objective, and risk tolerance. Some funds listed in the example may not be suitable for you. Dividends and capital gains distributions should be paid in cash if you need the income. Otherwise, have them reinvested in more shares of the mutual fund or another fund in the family.

FIGURE 17.10   Sample Portfolio Asset Allocation for a Retired Person over 65 Years of Age

Money Market Mutual Funds	15%
Bond Mutual Funds	50%
Stock Mutual Funds	35%

FIGURE 17.11   Sample Portfolio for a Person over 65 Years of Age

Money Market Mutual Funds:
   1 Money market fund

Bond Mutual Funds:
   1 Long-term government bond fund
   1 Long-term corporate bond fund (investment grade)
   1 Intermediate-term corporate bond fund (investment grade)
   1 Short-term corporate bond fund (investment grade)
   1 High-yield corporate bond fund (below investment grade)
   1 International bond fund–government and corporate
      (investment grade)

Stock Mutual Funds:
   1 Growth stock fund
   1 Growth and income stock fund
   1 Index stock fund
   1 Utility stock fund
   1 International stock fund–region

Growth-Oriented Portfolio

If you are growth-oriented you normally need to be invested in more stock funds than money market funds and bond funds. Therefore, you may want to have one money market fund, a few bond funds and the rest in stock funds.

If you fall in the category of a middle-aged person, your asset allocation may be the following as shown in Figure 17.12.

FIGURE 17.12   Sample Portfolio Asset Allocation for a Middle-Aged Person

Money Market Mutual Funds	10%
Bond Mutual Funds	25%
Stock Mutual Funds	65%

FIGURE 17.13   Sample Portfolio for a Middle-aged Person

Money Market Mutual Funds:
   1 Money market fund

Bond Mutual Funds:
   1 Municipal bond fund–state of residence, if applicable
   1 High-yield corporate bond fund (below investment grade)

Stock Mutual Funds:
   1 Aggressive growth stock fund
   2 Growth stock funds
   2 Growth and income stock funds
   1 Index fund
   1 Utility stock fund
   2 Sector or theme stock funds
   2 International stock funds–region or single country

Figure 17.13 shows the number and type of mutual funds for a portfolio for a middle-aged person.

The percent invested in each of the individual funds is dependent on your investor's profile, investment objective, and risk tolerance. Some funds listed in the example may not be suitable for you. Dividends and capital gains distributions should be reinvested in more shares of the mutual fund or another fund in the family.

If you fall in the category of a young person, your asset allocation may be the following as shown in Figure 17.14.

FIGURE 17.14   Sample Portfolio Asset Allocation for a Young Person

Money Market Mutual Funds	10%
Bond Mutual Funds	15%
Stock Mutual Funds	75%

FIGURE 17.15   Sample Portfolio for a Young Person

Money Market Mutual Funds:
  1 Money market fund

Bond Mutual Funds:
  1 High-yield corporate fund (below investment grade)

Stock Mutual Funds:
  2 Aggressive growth stock funds
  2 Growth stock funds
  2 Growth and income stock funds
  1 Index fund
  1 Utility stock fund
  2 Sector or theme stock funds
  2 International stock funds—region or single country

Figure 17.15 shows the number and type of mutual funds for a portfolio for a young person.

The percent invested in each of the individual funds is dependent on your investor's profile, investment objective, and risk tolerance. Some funds listed in the example may not be suitable for you. Dividends and capital gains distributions should be reinvested in more shares of the mutual fund or another fund in the family.

If you are investing for a child 12 years of age or under, your asset allocation may be the following as shown in Figure 17.16.

FIGURE 17.16   Sample Portfolio Asset Allocation for a Child 12 Years of Age or Under

Money Market Mutual Funds	10%
Bond Mutual Funds	10%
Stock Mutual Funds	80%

FIGURE 17.17   Sample Portfolio for a Child 12 Years of Age or Under

Money Market Mutual Funds:
  1 Money market fund

Bond Mutual Funds:
  1 Long-term government bond fund
  1 Intermediate corporate bond fund (investment grade)

Stock Mutual Funds:
  1 Growth stock fund
  2 Growth and income stock funds
  1 Index fund
  1 Utility stock fund
  2 Sector or theme stock funds
  1 International stock fund—region or single country

Figure 17.17 shows the number and type of mutual funds for a portfolio for a child 12 years of age or under.

The percent invested in each of the individual funds is dependent on the child's investor profile, investment objective, and risk tolerance. Some funds listed in the example may not be suitable for the child's portfolio. Dividends and capital gains distributions should be reinvested in more shares of the mutual fund or another fund in the family.

If you fall in the category of a high tax-bracket person, your asset allocation may be the following as shown in Figure 17.18.

FIGURE 17.18   Sample Portfolio Asset Allocation for a High Tax-Bracket Person

Money Market Mutual Funds	5%
Bond Mutual Funds	20%
Stock Mutual Funds	75%

FIGURE 17.19   Sample Portfolio for a High Tax-Bracket Person

Money Market Mutual Funds:
  1 Money market fund (tax-exempt)

Bond Mutual Funds:
  1 Municipal bond fund—state of residence, if applicable
  1 Municipal bond fund—national
  1 High-yield corporate bond fund (below investment grade)

Stock Mutual Funds:
  1 Aggressive growth stock fund
  2 Growth stock funds
  2 Growth and income stock funds
  1 Index fund
  2 Sector or theme stock funds
  2 International stock funds—region or single country

Figure 17.19 shows the number and type of mutual funds for a portfolio for a high tax-bracket person.

The percent invested in each of the individual funds is dependent on your investor's profile, investment objective, and risk tolerance. Some funds listed in the example may not be suitable for you. Dividends and capital gains distributions should be reinvested in more shares of the mutual fund or another fund in the family.

Complete Your Investor's Guide by listing the mutual fund management company and the number and types of mutual funds based on your investment policy statement.

Both dividends and capital gains distributions can significantly add to your total return. Your Investor's Guide provides a worksheet for keeping track of that distribution method you selected for your funds.

Market Timing versus Buy and Hold

Mutual funds are generally considered to be investments for the long term. Therefore, by definition you should select good quality mutual funds and hold them through the market cycles until your invest-

Your Investor's Guide

Management Company and Types of Mutual Funds

Mutual Fund Management Company _____

Money Market Mutual Funds:

1 _____

Bond Mutual Funds:

1 _____

1 _____

1 _____

1 _____

1 _____

1 _____

Stock Mutual Funds:

1 _____

1 _____

1 _____

1 _____

1 _____

1 _____

1 _____

1 _____

1 _____

1 _____

1 _____

1 _____

✎ **Your Investor's Guide**

Dividends and Capital Gains Distributions Selection

Mutual Fund Name _____

Distribution method selected:

Note: Check the line after "same fund," if applicable, or write in another fund's name on line after "another fund."

❑ 1. Receive both dividends and capital gains in cash.

❑ 2. Receive dividends in cash and reinvest capital gains in shares of the same fund ___or in shares of another fund _____ in the same family.

❑ 3. Reinvest the dividends in shares of the same fund ___or in shares of another fund _____ in the same family and receive the capital gains in cash.

❑ 4. Reinvest both dividends and capital gains in shares of the same fund ___ or in shares of another fund _____ in the same family.

---

ment objectives are met or they change. Because the stock market (and sometimes the bond market) is very volatile, it is difficult to trade effectively in and out and be consistently profitable over many years. Furthermore, the stock and bond markets sometimes perform extremely well during a short time period (several months) and then may not move significantly for many months. If you are not invested during a good-performing period, you miss a significant opportunity that could be the major part of that year's return.

Market Timing

Market timing means that you trade in and out of the market, attempting to always buy low and sell high. Therefore, when you try to time the market, you need to make three decisions:

1. The initial decision for the proper time to purchase a mutual fund

2. The decision for the proper time to sell the mutual fund
3. The decision for the proper time to buy back the mutual fund

Making all three decisions accurately and profitably is very difficult and time-consuming.

After you purchase a mutual fund, the share price may decline. At that time do you sell your shares to limit the loss, do you hold the shares, or do you purchase more shares at the lower price? Of course, after you purchase a mutual fund, the share price may rise. At that time do you sell your shares to realize a profit, do you hold the shares, or do you purchase more shares at the higher price because the market is rising? Once again you have to make several more decisions after your initial purchase when you are trying to time the market.

Whenever you sell (redeem) a mutual fund, even if it is considered an exchange for another fund when placing the order, a taxable event occurs for the sale. You either realize a profit or loss when you redeem a mutual fund. Therefore, when you are deciding to redeem (even via an exchange) a mutual fund, the tax liability (capital gains tax) may be a factor to consider.

Buy and Hold

The buy and hold strategy is usually the most appropriate for investors who want to achieve good long-term performance results.

However, some mutual funds do not perform as well as their respective fund group average or their appropriate market index. If the fund's performance is lacking after several years, it may be worthwhile to change from the under-performing fund to a better-performing fund. The fund's performance should not be judged over the short-term but rather over several market cycles.

Not all funds perform consistently and this year's best-performing funds may not be next year's best performing funds. *Contrarian investing* is investing in securities or mutual funds that are out of favor. Sometimes this year's poor-performing funds become next year's best-performing funds. The important point is purchasing and holding a mutual fund that is expected to meet your investment objective over your time horizon. You may want to consider dollar-cost-averaging investing and constant ratio investing. Refer to the glossary for definitions of these two terms.

Each strategy, market timing, buy and hold, dollar cost averaging, or constant ratio investing is based on your own personal preference, investment objectives, and risk tolerance. Your investment professional should be able to discuss with you the merits in further detail, or your readings or software program might lead you to a decision.

CHAPTER 18

Monitoring Your Mutual Fund's Performance

Because the stock and bond markets are always changing, you may need to review your mutual fund holdings periodically. Even though you may be a long-term investor, some funds may need to be sold and others bought as the marketplace shifts. Despite changing market conditions, performance of a particular fund also may dictate that you sell one fund for another. Using the exchange privilege within a family of funds usually eliminates any cost for making the transaction.

Performance Measurement

Performance may be measured in at least five ways:

1. Performance compared to your investment objective
2. Performance compared to an absolute number

3. Performance compared to a risk-free investment
4. Performance compared to a corresponding mutual fund index
5. Performance compared to a corresponding market average or index (benchmark)

Performance Compared to Your Investment Objective

Somewhere in the investing arena, someone is probably making a better return than you. However, you purchased a particular mutual fund for the purpose of obtaining a certain return. If you receive the expected return, then you should be satisfied with your mutual fund selection and its return. If you purchase an income fund and receive the income you anticipated, then your investment objective is met. If you purchase a growth fund and receive the capital appreciation you need, then your investment objective is met also. Not all investments meet our expectations, and that is why we phrase the expectation as only an investment objective.

Performance Compared to an Absolute Number

Performance, also known as *total return,* is the income plus any price appreciation or depreciation during a given time period. Normally, annualizing your return is the best method for calculating your return. If you are satisfied with your return, you have made a good investment decision. Trying to achieve a better return may require you to accept more risk than you want or can afford.

Performance Compared to a Risk-free Investment

The *risk-adjusted return* is your total return minus the return from a risk-free investment. A U.S. Treasury bill, considered the safest investment if held until maturity, is known as a risk-free investment. However, if you sell U.S. Treasury bills prior to maturity, you may experience a loss if interest rates increased significantly since your purchase. Many investors like to use a federally insured certificate of deposit (CD) as another risk-free investment comparison. Money market funds are essentially risk-free, especially government money market funds. However, money market funds are not insured or guaranteed; thus, they do carry some market risk. Your risk-adjusted return shows how much you gained above a risk-free investment.

If your risk-adjusted return is adequate for you based on the additional risks you take, then you made the right decision. However, if the added return is only a slightly increased return over the risk-free return, then you may want to consider selling your investment and purchasing a risk-free investment. Furthermore, if the added return is not sufficient for the risk taken, then you may want to consider selling your investment and purchasing another one with the same risk but a better potential return.

Performance Compared to a Corresponding Mutual Fund Index

Another way to measure performance is to compare your returns to other funds that are managed with the same investment objective and similar underlying securities, also known as a *universe*. Performing well in a particular segment of the market where all of the stocks in that segment are declining is very difficult. Therefore, it is beneficial to measure your fund's performance to the performance of other funds in the same market segment. If your fund is outperforming the other funds, then you should be satisfied. However, you need to determine that your fund is not assuming more risk than the other funds in the same universe. If so, you may want to find out why and whether the fund still meets your risk tolerance and investment objective. Your investment professional or your own research should be able to help you determine if the fund is just performing well or is assuming additional risk of which you are unaware.

If the fund is performing poorly relative to other funds, you may want to determine why and decide if you should move your assets to a better-performing fund. Mutual funds, like some of their underlying stocks and bonds, may perform on a cyclical basis. You don't want to sell a fund at a low point just prior to having the fund make a significant return on the upside. Many times contrarian investing (buying mutual funds when they are out of favor) turns out to be a profitable investment decision. Refer to Chapter 9 for appropriate mutual fund indexes to use for performance comparisons.

Performance Compared to a Market Average or Index (Benchmark)

Indexes, also known as *benchmarks,* help you compare your mutual fund's performance because your fund can only perform as well as the weighted average of the underlying securities. An *index* or *average* represents a universe of selected securities that are similar as measured by some recognized criteria. Most mutual fund portfolio managers try to beat a comparable index each year. Indexes and averages are difficult to beat because the index or average does not have any management fees or expenses. Indexes and averages are considered passive because they are reflective, not managed. An index or average represents the same or similar securities. Periodically, based on the criteria used for the selection of the securities, securities are added to or withdrawn from the universe of the index or average. The process of changing securities in an index or average is known as *rebalancing* or *reconstituting.* The difficult part of using an index or average for comparison purposes is selecting the most comparable index or average. Many may seem appropriate but the securities in the mutual fund's portfolio may not be reflected in the underlying components in the index or average. Comparing your mutual fund to several indexes or averages may give you a better indication of your fund's performance. Refer to Chapter 9 for appropriate market indexes and averages to use for performance comparisons.

Northwest Quadrant

Each mutual fund can be plotted on a graph showing its rate of return and its risk. The rate of return figure can represent any period of time, such as one year, three years, five years, ten years, or longer. The rate of return is the total return that includes capital gain or loss, plus income earned. The risk is the standard deviation of the return. In theory, the higher the risk of the investment the greater *potential* for a higher return. Those mutual funds that appear in the upper left corner, known as the *northwest quadrant,* provide you with the possibility of the highest return with the least amount of risk. Figure 18.1 shows the four quadrants of rates of return and risk.

FIGURE 18.1 Quadrants of Rates of Return and Risk

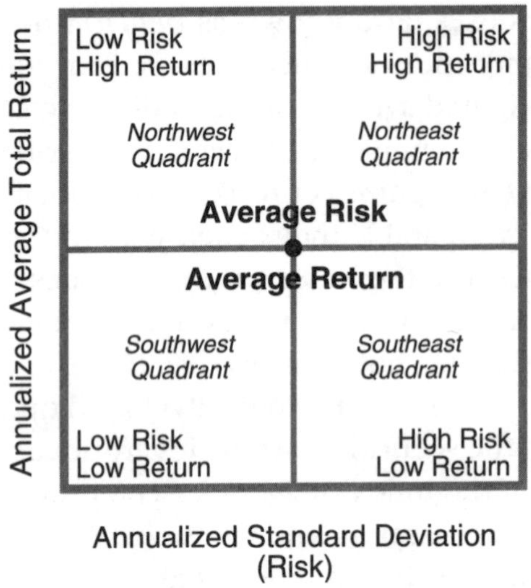

Comparing Dividends and Total Returns

 Many management companies offer fund shares with different types of cost structures, such as a front-end sales charge, a contingent deferred sales charge, a level-load, and a no-load. The types of cost structures generally are described by a class designation (Class A, Class B, Class C, or Class I, Class II, etc.). You may purchase the same fund by selecting a specific share class. A mutual fund that offers multiple classes of shares is sometimes called a *multi-class fund*. A fund that offers only one share class is sometimes called a *single-class fund*.

 Typically, each share class of the same fund incurs different annual operating expenses, such as management feees, 12b-1 fees, and other expenses, along with applicable sales charges, if any. A fund distributes net investment income, the fund's income after operating expenses. For each share class, dividends may vary depending on the operating expenses of the respective share class. Because dividends may vary for each share class, yield and distribution rates may be different. Likewise, the fund's total return may vary for each share class, depending on the fund's operating expenses, length of time shares are held, and applicable sales charges, if any.

Understanding Tax Issues

Taxation can reduce your investment return significantly. Knowing the impact of taxation may help you reduce the adverse effect from taxation.

The mutual fund management company or transfer agent sends you the appropriate tax information to assist you in completing your annual tax return. Some of the forms and statements which you may receive are:

- Form 1099-DIV Dividends and Distributions
- Tax-exempt summary statement
- Form 1099-B Proceeds from Broker and Barter Exchange Transactions
- Cost basis statement
- Year-end statement

The following IRS Publications may help you further understand taxation of mutual funds:

- Publication 564 *Mutual Fund Distributions*
- Publication 550 *Investment Income and Expenses*

- Publication 525 *Taxable and Nontaxable Income*
- Publication 909 *Alternative Minimum Tax for Individuals*
- Publication 514 *Foreign Tax Credit for Individuals*

Because every city and state has different tax regulations, they are not discussed here. Consult with your tax adviser or the IRS for advice regarding the taxation of mutual funds distributions and redemptions (sales).

Distributions

Mutual fund distributions may consist of the following five items:

1. Taxable dividends
2. Tax-exempt dividends
3. Short-term capital gains
4. Long-term capital gains
5. Nontaxable distributions

Note that for tax purposes, any dividends and capital gains declared during the last quarter of any calendar year that are paid before February 1 the following calendar year are deemed to have been received by the shareholder in the prior year.

Taxable dividends. Taxable dividends are paid to you when the fund earns taxable income from its underlying securities. The fund pays you substantially all of its *net investment income*–income after expenses. If the fund earns income from cash dividends (stocks) or taxable interest (debt securities), then the income paid to you is declared a taxable dividend.

Net short-term capital gains are paid to you when the fund realizes net short-term capital gains from securities that the fund held one year or less. *Net short-term capital gains* is calculated by subtracting short-term capital losses from short-term capital gains. Each year the fund pays you substantially all of its realized net short-term capital gains. The IRS taxes your short-term capital gains as ordinary income.

The IRS considers a taxable dividend as ordinary income, whether you receive the taxable dividend distribution in cash or reinvest it in additional shares of the fund.

Tax-exempt dividends. Tax-exempt dividends are paid to you when the fund earns tax-exempt income from its underlying securities. Each year the fund pays you substantially all of its net investment income. *Net investment income* is calculated by subtracting the fund's expenses from the investment income. If the fund earns income from tax-exempt interest (debt securities), then the income paid to you is declared a tax-exempt dividend. The IRS considers a tax-exempt dividend as reportable but not necessarily taxable, whether you receive the taxable dividend distribution in cash or reinvest it in additional shares of the fund. However, if all or a portion of the tax-exempt distribution contains interest from a bond considered to be an alternative minimum tax (AMT) issue, then that portion may be subject to the alternative minimum tax. Refer to the glossary for a definition of AMT.

Private purpose bonds, also known as *private activity bonds,* are municipal bonds where a portion of the proceeds are used for private activities, such as sports and convention facilities, and large industrial developments. While most taxpayers are not subject to alternative minimum tax, bond interest received from private purpose bonds is added to the alternative minimum tax calculation. If your mutual fund holds AMT bonds, then the portion of the net investment income from these bonds must be included on the AMT tax form.

Long-term capital gains. Long-term capital gains are paid to you when the fund realizes net long-term capital gains from securities that the fund held for more than one year. *Net long-term capital gains* is calculated by subtracting long-term capital losses from long-term capital gains. The IRS considers long-term capital gains as capital gains distributions.

Long-term capital gains in this context refers to the trading activity within the fund's portfolio. You should generally treat any long-term capital gains distribution as long term, regardless of how long you have held the fund's shares.

Nontaxable distributions. In some cases the mutual fund pays you a nontaxable distribution such as a return of principal. A *return of principal* is paid when a fund pays distributions from sources other than from net investment income, net realized short-term capital gains, or net realized long-term capital gains. The IRS does not consider the distribution as ordinary income or capital gains. However, you must reduce the cost basis of your fund shares by the amount of the nontaxable distribution. Therefore, when you redeem the fund's shares, you will either have a larger capital gain or a smaller capital loss due to a lower cost basis. If your cost basis is reduced to zero, a return of principal distribution is then considered a capital gain and must be reported accordingly, even if Form 1099-DIV shows it as a nontaxable distribution.

Reclassification of dividends. After a mutual fund has paid you distributions, it may be necessary to reclassify the distribution. Reclassifying dividends can occur when a fund pays out more income than it actually earned during the year. Audits performed following the close of a fund's fiscal year may determine that the fund made an overpayment. Therefore, the fund must reclassify the overpayment as a return of principal. In this case, the redesignation means you are receiving your invested principal and according to federal tax laws the IRS requires you to reduce your cost basis by the amount of this type of reclassified dividend.

Another circumstance that could result in a reclassification is net foreign currency gains or losses. Net foreign currency gains and losses may result in an addition to, or charge against, net investment income. As a result of net currency losses in a fund's portfolio for its respective fiscal year, a portion of the dividends paid may be redesignated as nontaxable return of principal. The IRS does not require you to reduce your cost basis by the amount of this type of reclassified dividend.

Form 1099-DIV Dividends and Distributions

IRS *Form 1099-DIV* reports your mutual funds dividends and distributions during the preceding year. Whether you received the distributions in cash or reinvested them, the IRS considers that you received it and it must be reported accordingly. For tax purposes, any distributions declared during the last quarter of any calendar year that are paid prior to February 1 the following calendar year are deemed to have been received by the shareholder in the prior year. The form also displays your name, Social Security number or tax identification number (TIN), fund's name, and other information.

Gross dividends and other distributions on stock. Box 1a of IRS Form 1099-DIV reports your total *Gross Dividends and Other Distributions on Stock.* This section reports the total distributions paid to you. This figure is then broken down into specific tax categories.

Ordinary dividends. Box 1b of IRS Form 1099-DIV reports your *Ordinary Dividends,* which includes the sum of your taxable dividends, taxable interest, and short-term capital gains.

Capital gains distributions. Box 1c of IRS Form 1099-DIV reports your *Capital Gains Distributions,* which are considered long-term capital gains distributions.

Federal income tax withheld. Box 2 of IRS Form 1099-DIV reports *Federal Income Tax Withheld.* Additionally, if you have not furnished a signed IRS *Form W-9 Request for Taxpayer Identification Number and Certification* certifying your Social Security number or TIN to your brokerage firm or mutual fund's transfer agent, you may be subject to 31 percent federal income backup withholding tax on taxable dividends, capital gains distributions, and the proceeds from redemptions (sales). Once the financial institution withholds and pays the IRS the federal backup withholding tax, the financial institution may not return the tax to you. However, you may use the amount of the federal backup withholding tax paid to the IRS as a credit toward payment of your federal income tax for that year. When you receive your first mutual fund or brokerage firm statement, check for the accuracy of your Social Security number or tax identification number.

Foreign tax paid. Box 3 of IRS Form 1099-DIV reports *Foreign Tax Paid.* Mutual funds that invest in foreign stocks and bonds may receive dividends and interest from foreign companies. The fund must pay taxes to the appropriate countries on the dividends and interest. The foreign tax payment is usually considered a fund's expense. If, as of year-end, a fund has more than 50 percent of its assets invested in foreign securities, the fund may elect to pass through this expense to you. You may take the amount of foreign tax withheld as either a foreign tax credit by filing IRS Form 1116 *Foreign Tax Credit* or as an itemized deduction on

Schedule A. Otherwise, the fund may deduct the foreign tax in calculating the amount of its income distribution.

Tax-Exempt Summary Statement

A tax-exempt summary statement, sometimes called a *tax-savings report,* provides you with the amount of tax-exempt dividends paid to you during the year. Even if the income is not taxed, it is reportable on your tax return.

Estimated Year-End Distributions

Some mutual fund companies provide estimated year-end distributions. The benefit of receiving the information is that if you are contemplating purchasing shares of a mutual fund near year-end, then you are better prepared for year-end tax planning. For example, if you purchase shares of a fund in early December and the fund pays a substantial long-term capital gains distribution in late December, you are liable for the tax due on the distribution even though you have held the shares less than a month. Depending on the market conditions and your tax situation, you may want to defer your purchase until after the capital gains distribution has been paid. However, you run the risk of buying the shares later at a higher price, which may offset any tax-savings.

Share Redemptions

When you sell shares of a mutual fund, you have a reportable transaction for tax purposes, a capital gain, capital loss, or break-even.

Form 1099-B Proceeds from Broker and Barter Exchange Transactions

If you redeem shares of a mutual fund, the mutual fund company must report the gross sale proceeds to the IRS and to you on *Form 1099-B Proceeds from Broker and Barter Exchange Transactions. Gross sale proceeds* is the total amount of sale proceeds (redemptions) you received during the year. The company does not report your basis or your gain or loss to the IRS. You must report both the buy and sell transactions on *Form 1040 Schedule D Capital Gains and Losses.* The amount of the cost basis of the shares is subtracted from the amount of sale proceeds to determine your capital gain or loss. Furthermore, the IRS checks your tax return against the gross sale proceeds figure that was sent to them by the mutual fund company. Therefore, it is imperative for you to report all of your transactions each year.

In addition to selling your shares for cash, exchanging your shares from one fund to another fund constitutes a sale and a new buy. The sale from the exchange has to be reported on your *Form 1040 Schedule D Capital Gains and Losses.* Shares sold that were acquired from reinvested dividends and capital gains distributions also are subject to report. Of course, transactions in a qualified retirement account, such as an individual retirement account or pension plan, are exempt from report.

Calculating Your Basis

The *basis* is the amount you paid for all shares including shares purchased through dividend and capital gains distributions reinvestment. When you redeem all of your shares or a portion of your shares, you must calculate the basis for the shares sold. Several methods are acceptable by the IRS when you calculate your basis such as cost basis or average basis. Remember, once you have selected a method in regards to a particular mutual fund, you must use the same method until all of the shares in that fund are sold. In order to change methods, you must receive the consent from the Commissioner of the Internal Revenue Service. However, you may use different methods for different funds.

Many mutual fund companies are providing shareholders with cost basis statements that give you the cost basis for shares purchased recently. In some cases, the statement provides the cost basis for shares purchased in prior years. However, you are still responsible for the accuracy of the information you file on your tax return.

Cost basis. Under the cost basis, two methods are available: (1) first-in, first-out (FIFO) and (2) specific share identification.

First-in, first-out method. The first-in, first-out method means that you are selling the first shares that you purchased. Subsequent sales represent the next shares that you purchased, and so on, until you have sold all of your shares.

Specific share identification method. The specific share identification method means that you designate which shares you are selling. Therefore, you may determine the amount of capital gain or capital loss by selecting which shares you are selling. However, you must tell your investment professional or write to the mutual fund's transfer agent stating the purchase date of the shares being sold so they can confirm your specification in writing within a reasonable time.

Average basis. Under the average basis, two methods are available: (1) single-category and (2) double-category. In order for you to use the average basis method, your shares must be on deposit in an account handled by a custodian or agent who purchases, redeems, or exchanges shares on your behalf. Therefore, if you hold shares in certificate form, you may not use the average cost method for those shares.

Single-category method. In the single-category method, you find the average cost of all shares owned at the time of each sale, regardless of how long you owned them. Include shares purchased with reinvested dividends and capital gains distributions. To calculate the basis of the shares sold, you add the cost of all shares owned, then divide the cost of all shares by the number of shares owned. The result is your average basis per share. Then multiply the average basis per share by the number of shares sold. The basis of your shares determined under average basis is the basis of all of your shares in the account at the time of each sale. You average basis per share changes as you make additional purchases and reinvest dividends and capital gains distributions.

Double-category method. All shares in an account at the time of each sale are divided into two categories: short term and long term. Shares held one year or less are short term. Shares held longer than one year are long-term. The basis of each share in a category is the total basis of all shares in that category at the time of sale, divided by the total shares in the category. To determine the basis for shares acquired by gift or inheritance, refer to IRS Publication 564 *Mutual Fund Distributions* or see your tax adviser.

Year-End Statement

The mutual fund company provides you with a year-end statement showing the beginning share balance, purchases, sales, shares purchased from reinvested dividends, and ending share balance. In addition, the statement gives you total distributions, your dividend payment method, the number of shares held by you in certificate form, and the number of shares held at the mutual fund company's transfer agent.

Mutual fund companies usually send you monthly or quarterly statements. These interim statements can usually be discarded when you get the year-end statement. The year-end statement is normally a cumulative statement showing the whole year's activity. Keeping all of the year-end statements, in addition to your cost basis statements, is important for your tax records.

Cost of Taxation

Your investment return is reduced by the amount of tax you pay on the return. When you sell shares and realize a long-term capital gain, you may pay a capital gains tax. Likewise, when you receive taxable dividends, you may pay an income tax. Considering the impact of taxation is important when buying and selling mutual funds. Your investment decision to buy a specific fund or sell a fund at a particular time usually is more important than the tax consideration. However, you calculate the impact of taxation prior to making an investment decision.

A Personal Note

The *Mutual Fund Kit* has provided information and strategies to help you build a mutual fund portfolio that will meet your investment objectives and fit your investor's profile.

If you do your homework and receive good advice before you invest, believe in yourself and let your investments work for you. A good, sound investment portfolio will add satisfaction to your life and hopefully provide financial security for you and those you love.

Appendix A

Your Portfolio Investment Questions (PIQs)

Many financial newspapers, magazines, and brokerage firm recommendations refer to mutual funds. With more than 10,000 individual funds to select from nationwide, trying to know and understand their investment objectives, sales charges, expenses, 12b-1 distribution fees, underlying securities, asset allocation, and other pertinent information is quite a job. The following PIQs should help you begin the process of selecting suitable investments for your portfolio. If and when you add any mutual funds to your portfolio, complete a PIQs form for each one. This will help you organize your investments by asset allocation and types of investment objectives. Knowing this information about each of your mutual funds also will help you decide when to make additional investments in a fund, based on current or projected market conditions.

Your Portfolio Investment Questions (PIQs)

Name of Mutual Fund _____ Date _____

From where may I obtain a current prospectus, research report, and/or annual report?

Name _____

Firm _____

Address _____ Telephone Number _____

_____ Fax Number _____

What is the type of mutual fund? Check one.

❑ U.S. Long-Term Bond, Taxable

❑ U.S. Intermediate-Term Bond, Taxable

❑ U.S. Short-Term Bond, Taxable

❑ U.S. Long-Term Bond, Tax-Exempt

❑ U.S. Intermediate-Term Bond, Tax-Exempt

- ❏ U.S. Short-Term Bond, Tax-Exempt
- ❏ Global Long-Term Bond
- ❏ Global Intermediate-Term Bond
- ❏ Global Short-Term Bond
- ❏ International Long-Term Bond
- ❏ International Intermediate-Term Bond
- ❏ International Short-Term Bond
- ❏ U.S. Stock
- ❏ U.S. Balanced
- ❏ Global Balanced
- ❏ Asset Allocation
- ❏ International Stock
- ❏ Global Stock
- ❏ International Balanced
- ❏ Other _____

What is the fund's investment objective?

What securities may the fund purchase?

What is the average quality of the underlying securities currently being held in the mutual fund?

Who is the portfolio manager?

How long has the current portfolio manager been managing the fund?

What has been the total return of the fund for the past one, three, five, and ten years?

What is the SEC Yield?

What is the current distribution rate?

Is the dividend distribution taxable or tax-exempt?

What is the net asset value (NAV)?

What is the offering price?

What type of pricing structure is the fund? Check one.

- ❑ Front-End Sales Charge (FESC)
- ❑ Contingent Deferred Sales Charge (CDSC)
- ❑ Level-load (LL)
- ❑ Institutional
- ❑ No-load (NL)

What are the sales charges for buying the shares?

What are the sales charges or fees for selling the shares?

What are the total operating expenses?

What is the procedure for reinvesting dividends and capital gains?

What is the procedure and cost for the exchange privilege?

Which mutual fund index is appropriate for comparing the fund's performance?

Which market index or average is appropriate for comparing the fund's performance?

What economic scenario could cause the net asset value to increase?

What economic scenario could cause the net asset value to decrease?

The shares of the mutual fund will be (check one)

- ❑ issued in certificate form to me.
- ❑ held at the mutual fund's transfer agent.
- ❑ held in street name in my brokerage account.

What is the fund's symbol?

Appendix B

Financial Focuses

Financial Focus 1—Model Portfolio Allocation Solely Based on Age

You can structure your mutual fund portfolio in many different ways. A basic portfolio approach is to allocate your assets among the three categories—money market funds, bond funds, and stock funds. The percentage placed in each category is based on your age. The percent of your assets to be invested in bond and money market funds is approximately your age. The remainder percentage (100 minus your age) may be invested in stock funds. The amount and types of money market funds, bond funds, and stock funds depends on your Investment Policy Statement. As you grow older, the percentages change and you adjust your portfolio accordingly. This portfolio approach as shown in Figure B.1 is only suitable if it meets with your overall investment objectives, risk tolerance, and financial situation.

Financial Focus 2—Why Bond Prices Change

One of the hardest concepts to understand is why bond and note prices change. Two basic features that most bonds and notes have are a fixed interest rate (coupon rate) and a fixed maturity date.

Bond and note prices change when interest rates fluctuate in the marketplace. You need to know that *bond and note prices decrease as interest rates rise,* and *bond and note prices increase as interest rates fall.* If you hold the bond or note to maturity and the issuer has sufficient cash (in the case of corporate or municipal bonds and notes), you will receive par value ($1,000 per bond or note). Even if the bond or note fluctuates while you are holding it, you will receive $1,000 (par value) per bond or note if you keep it until maturity (assuming the issuer has the financial means to pay the debt at maturity).

FIGURE B.1   A Portfolio Model Based Solely on Age

Age	Stock Funds	Bond and Money Market Funds
25	75%	25%
30	70	30
35	65	35
40	60	40
45	55	45
50	50	50
55	45	55
60	40	60
65	35	65
70	30	70
75	25	75
80	20	80
85	15	85
90	10	90
95	5	95

This model adjusts for your perceived income and capital growth needs and your risk tolerance at certain ages without requiring a lot of time to oversee your investment. Obviously, the more simple a strategy, the less it is tailored to you.

Some economic variables that cause interest rates to change are credit demands for money, inflation, unemployment or full employment, recession, economic expansion, political environment, Federal Reserve Bank (Fed) policies, change in tax laws, and government spending. The Federal Reserve Bank, the U.S. monetary agent, adjusts interest rates to try to control inflation and economic growth. Congress, the U.S. fiscal agent, controls taxes and government spending, which directly affects the growth of the U.S. economy.

Existing bonds compete for investors with new bonds being issued both on current yield and yield-to-maturity. As new bonds are issued during time of fluctuating interest rates, the only thing that can change on an existing fixed-rate bond to compete with new bonds is the market price. Consequently, the changing market price provides revised yields, which are now competitive with the yields on new bonds.

For example, *today* you buy a $1,000 U.S. Treasury bond with 9 percent due 10/01/2018 for $1,000. Your cost is $1,000 and you receive income of $90 per year until 10/01/2018. Therefore, your current yield today is 9 percent ($90 ÷ $1,000 × 100).

One month later the Federal Reserve Bank raises interest rates and the U.S. government issues a new bond, such as a U.S. Treasury bond 10 percent due 11/01/2018 at $1,000. If you want to sell your bond, how much is it worth in the marketplace? Another investor could buy the new bond and receive $100 per year until 11/01/2018 (a 10 percent current yield), or the person could buy your bond depending on the market price.

For the other investor to receive a 10 percent current yield from your bond, the person would pay you $900. To determine the price of $900, simply divide the income of $90 by 10 percent (the current yield). The other investor could buy your bond for $900 and receive $90, or buy the new bond for $1,000 and receive $100. Either way, the other investor has the opportunity to earn a 10 percent current yield from either bond. *As you can see, when interest rates rise, bond prices decrease. When interest rates fall, bond prices increase.*

In the above example, the change of interest rate of 1 percent in one month is only for illustration purposes. Also, the level of yields to maturity for other bonds may affect the market price and cause your bond to trade higher or lower than $900.

When interest rates change, longer-term bonds and notes normally fluctuate more than shorter-term bonds and notes because the effect of the change is longer-lasting. Therefore, the best time to buy long-term bonds may be when long-term interest rates are high and are expected to fall. The best time to buy short-term notes may be when long-term rates are low and are expected to rise.

Financial Focus 3—Brief Overview of International Economics

A difficult concept to understand is the economic impact of foreign currency changes relative to the U.S. dollar or other currencies. Foreign currency exchange rates change daily, which impacts valuations of securities, balance of trade, and balance of payments. *Balance of payments* is a system for recording all of a country's economic transactions with the rest of the world during a particular time period. *Balance of trade* is the net difference over a period of time between the value of a country's imports and the value of its exports of merchandise. A positive balance of trade means a country sold more goods than it bought—in adjusted currency. A negative balance of trade means it bought more than it sold—in adjusted currency. (*Barron's Finance & Investment Handbook.*)

Simply stated, when the value of the U.S. dollar rises against the value of a foreign currency, the foreign country's economic condition is more competitive. The demand for foreign merchandise increases because the U.S. dollar buys more foreign merchandise, thus the foreign country's economy benefits. The demand for U.S. merchandise decreases because the foreign currency buys less U.S. products, thus hurting the U.S. economy. Therefore, the foreign country typically exports more and imports less merchandise, and the United States exports less and imports more merchandise. The expanding foreign economy may help the valuation of the foreign country's stocks. The weaker U.S. economy may hurt the valuation of U.S. stocks. As the value of the U.S. dollar reverses and becomes weaker, the export–import balance reverses. The United States begins to export less and imports more merchandise and the foreign country exports more and imports less merchandise. The stronger U.S. economy may help increase the valuation of U.S. stocks. The weaker foreign country's economy may hurt the valuation of the foreign country's stocks.

As the United States attracts more buyers for its merchandise and imports increase, the prices of the merchandise increase. As prices increase, the demand for the U.S. merchandise decreases and the exports decrease.

Likewise, as demand for foreign merchandise increases, the foreign country's exports increase. As prices rise, the demand for merchandise falls, which causes the foreign country's exports to decline.

A strong U.S. dollar may be good for domestic bond prices because a strong U.S. dollar fights inflation, thus keeping interest rates low. A weak U.S. dollar may be poor for domestic bond prices because a weak dollar may allow inflation to increase, thus keeping pressure on for higher interest rates.

In summary, when the foreign exchange rates move and demand for merchandise changes, a country's balance of trade position changes. If a country exports more merchandise than it imports, the country has a *balance of trade surplus.* If a country imports more merchandise than it exports, the country has a *balance of trade deficit.*

If a U.S. investor buys securities of a foreign country and subsequently the U.S. dollar falls against the foreign country's currency, when the security is sold and the foreign currency is converted back into U.S. dollars, the investor realizes a profit from the foreign exchange conversion. The foreign currency exchange profit is then added to the profit or loss from the security's market price movement.

If a U.S. investor buys securities of a foreign country and subsequently the U.S. dollar rises against the foreign country's currency, when the security is sold and the foreign currency is converted back into U.S. dollars, the investor realizes a loss from the foreign exchange conversion. The foreign currency exchange loss is then added to the profit or loss from the security's market price movement.

Investing in international and global mutual funds carries foreign exchange currency risk. The net asset value (NAV) of your fund shares may decline if the value of the foreign currencies represented by the underlying securities decline against the value of the U.S. dollar. The NAV of your fund shares may increase if the value of the foreign currencies represented by the underlying securities rise against the value of the U.S. dollar. The amount of risk is dependent on the volatility of the currency represented in the portfolio, and the amount of currency hedging the portfolio manager employs (see Chapter 6).

Appendix C

Tax Information Form

Purchase Information (Complete where applicable)

Name of Mutual Fund _____

Type of Mutual Fund _____

Investment Professional _____

Firm Purchased Through _____

Address _____

_____

Telephone Number _____ Fax _____

CUSIP Number _____ Symbol _____

Trade Date _____ Settlement Date _____

Shares Purchased _____

Purchase Price $_____ Total Basis $_____

Subsequent Information

Date you established Reinvestment Plan–Dividends _____

(retain all year-end statements)   Short-Term Capital Gains _____

Long-Term Capital Gains _____

Sale Information

Trade Date _____   Settlement Date _____

Shares Sold _____   NAV $_____

Net Proceeds $_____
(net proceeds equals NAV times shares minus sales charge, if any)

Profit or Loss $ _____ *(net proceeds minus total basis)*

Method Used for Calculating Your Basis_____

Appendix D

Resources

Industry Organizations

American Stock Exchange (AMEX)
86 Trinity Place
New York, NY 10006-1881
212-306-1000
http://www.amex.com

Association for Investment Management and Research (AIMR)
5 Boar's Head Lane
P.O. Box 3668
Charlottesville, VA 22903-0668
804-980-3668; 800-247-8132
http://www.aimr.org

Investment Company Institute
1401 H Street, N.W., Suite 1200
Washington, DC 20005-2148
202-326-5800
http://www.ici.org

National Association of Securities Dealers, Inc. (NASD)
1735 K Street, N.W.
Washington, DC 20006-1506
301-590-6500
http://www.nasd.com

New York Stock Exchange
11 Wall Street
New York, NY 10005
212-656-3000
http://www.nyse.com

Research Services Firms

The Bond Buyer
One State Street Plaza, Floor 26
New York, NY 10004
212-803-8200; 800-982-0633
http://www.bondbuyer.com

CDA/Wiesenberger
1355 Piccard Drive
Rockville, MD 20850
301-975-9600; 800-232-2285
http://www.cda.com

Chase Global Data and Research
73 Junction Square
Concord, MA 01742
800-639-9494
http://www.chaseglobaldata.com

DALBAR, Inc.
Federal Reserve Plaza, Floor 30
600 Atlantic Avenue
Boston, MA 02210-2226
617-723-6400; 800-296-7056
http://www.dalbar.com

Dow Jones & Company
World Financial Center
200 Liberty Street
New York, NY 10281-1003
212-416-2000; 800-568-7625
http://www.dowjones.com

Ibbotson Associates
225 North Michigan Avenue, Suite 700
Chicago, IL 60601-7676
312-616-1620; 800-758-3557
http://www.ibbotson.com

IBC Financial Data, Inc.
290 Eliot Street
P.O. Box 9104
Ashland, MA 01721-9104
508-881-2800
http://www.ibcdata.com

I/B/E/S International Inc.
One World Trade Center, Floor 18
New York, NY 10048-1818
212-437-8200
http://www.ibes.com

Lipper Analytical Service, Inc.
47 Maple Street
Summit, NJ 07901-2571
908-598-2220
http://www.lipperweb.com

Moody's Investors Service, Inc.
99 Church Street
New York, NY 10007-2701
212-553-0300; 800-342-5647 Ext. 0546
http://www.moodys.com

Morningstar, Inc.
225 West Wacker Drive
Chicago, IL 60606-1224
312-424-4288; 800-735-0700
http://www.morningstar.net

Frank Russell Company
P.O. Box 1616
909 A Street
Tacoma, WA 98401-1616
206-572-9500
http://www.russell.com

Standard & Poor's
25 Broadway
New York, NY 10004-1010
212-208-8000; 800-221-5277
Ratings: http://www.ratings.standardpoor.com/
 funds
Equities: http://
 www.stockinfo.standardpoor.com

Value Line Publishing, Inc.
220 East 42nd Street
New York, NY 10017-5891
212-907-1500; 800-634-3583
http://www.valueline.com

Wilshire Associates
1299 Ocean Avenue
Santa Monica, CA 90401-1085
310-451-3051
http://www.wilshire.com

Newspapers

Barron's
Investor's Business Daily
The New York Times

The Wall Street Journal
USA Today

Books

Barron's Finance and Investment Handbook, by
John Downes and Jordan Elliott Goodman
(Barron's Educational Series, Inc.)

Building Your Mutual Fund Portfolio, by Albert
J. Fredman and Russ Wiles (Dearborn Financial
Publishing, Inc.)

*Business Week: The Insider's Guide to Mutual
Funds* (McGraw-Hill, Inc.)

Everyone's Money Book, by Jordan E. Goodman
(Dearborn Financial Publishing, Inc.)

The Investing Kit, by Bay Gruber (Dearborn
Financial Publishing, Inc.)

The Personal Finance Kit, by Ellen Norris Gruber
(Dearborn Financial Publishing, Inc.)

*The Wall Street Journal Guide to Understanding
Money & Investing,* by Kenneth M. Morris and
Alan M. Siegel (Lightbulb Press/Fireside/Simon &
Schuster, Inc.)

Glossary

Special appreciation is extended to Dearborn's Securities Product Development for assisting me in compiling this glossary.

adjusted basis   The value attributed to an asset or security that reflects any deductions taken on, or capital improvements to, the asset or security. Adjusted basis is used to compute the gain or loss on the sale or other disposition of the asset or security.

agency issue   A debt security issued by an authorized agency of the federal government. Such issues are backed by the issuing agencies themselves, not by the full faith and credit of the U.S. government (except GNMA and Federal Import Export Bank issues). *See also* government security

alternative minimum tax (AMT)   An alternative tax computation that adds certain tax preference items back into adjusted gross income. If the AMT is higher than the regular tax liability for the year, the regular tax and the amount by which the AMT exceeds the regular tax are paid. *See also* tax preference item

American depositary receipt (ADR)   A negotiable certificate representing a given number of shares of stock in a foreign corporation; it is bought and sold in the American securities markets, just as stock is traded.

basis   The cost of an asset or security

basis point   A measure of a bond's yield, equal to $\frac{1}{100}$ of 1 percent of yield. A bond whose yield increases from 5 percent to 5.5 percent is said to increase by 50 basis points. *See also* point

bear market   A market in which prices of a certain group of securities are falling or are expected to fall. *See also* bull market

blue chip stock   The equity issues of financially stable, well-established companies that have demonstrated their ability to pay dividends in both good and bad times.

bond   A legal obligation of an issuing company or government to repay the principal of a loan to bond investors at a specified future date. Bonds are usually issued with a par value or face value of $1,000, representing the amount of money borrowed. The issuer promises to pay a percentage of the par value as interest on the borrowed funds. The interest payment is stated on the face of the bond at issue.

bond interest coverage ratio   An indication of the safety of a corporate bond. It measures the number of times by which earnings before interest and taxes exceeds annual interest on outstanding bonds.

bond quote   One of a number of quotations listed in the financial press and most daily newspapers that provide representative bid prices from the previous day's bond market. Quotes for corporate and government bonds are percentages of the bond's face value (usually $1,000). Corporate bonds are quoted in increments of $\frac{1}{8}$, where a quote $99\frac{1}{8}$ represents 99.125 percent of par, or $991.25. Government bonds are quoted in $\frac{1}{32}$. Municipal bonds may be quoted on a dollar basis or on a yield-to-maturity basis.

bond yield   The annual rate of return on a bond investment. Types of yield include nominal yield, current yield, yield to maturity, and yield to call. Their relationships vary according to whether the bond in question is at a discount, at a premium, or at par. *See also* current yield; nominal yield; yield to call; yield to maturity

book value per share   A measure of the net worth of each share of common stock. It is calculated by subtracting intangible assets and preferred stock from total net worth and then dividing the result by the number of shares of common stock outstanding.

bull market   A market in which prices of a certain group of securities are rising or are expected to rise. *See also* bear market

business cycle   A predictable long-term pattern of alternating periods of economic growth and decline. The cycle passes through four stages: expansion, peak, contraction, and trough.

business day   A day on which financial markets are open for trading. Saturdays, Sundays, and legal holidays are not considered business days.

callable bond   A type of bond issued with a provision allowing the issuer to redeem the bond prior to maturity at a predetermined price. *See also* call price

callable preferred stock   A type of preferred stock issued with a provision allowing the corporation to call in the stock at a certain price and retire it. *See also* call price; preferred stock

call date   The date, specified in the prospectus of every callable security, after which the issuer of the security has the option to redeem the issue at the par or at par plus a premium.

call feature   *See* call provision.

call price   The price (usually a premium over the par value of the issue) at which preferred stocks or bonds can be redeemed prior to maturity of the issue.

call protection   A provision in a bond indenture stating that the issue is noncallable for a certain period of time (five years, ten years, etc.) after the original issue date. *See also* call provision

call provision   The written agreement between an issuing corporation and its bondholders or preferred stockholders, giving the corporation the option to redeem its senior securities at a specified price before maturity and under specified conditions.

call risk   The potential for a bond to be called before maturity, leaving the investor without the bond's current income. As this is more likely to occur during times of falling interest rates, the investor may not be able to reinvest his or her principal at a comparable rate of return.

capital appreciation   A rise in the market price of an asset.

capital gain   The profit realized when a capital asset is sold for a higher price than the purchase price.

capital loss   The loss incurred when a capital asset is sold for a lower price than the purchase price.

capital market   The segment of the securities market that deals in instruments with more than one year to maturity—that is, long-term debt and equity securities.

cash dividend   Money paid to a corporation's shareholders out of the corporation's current earnings or accumulated profits. All dividends must be declared by the board of directors.

cash equivalent   A security that can be readily converted into cash; examples include Treasury bills, certificates of deposit, and money market instruments and funds.

cash flow   The money received by a business minus the money paid out. Cash flow is also equal to net income plus depreciation or depletion.

coincident indicator   A measurable economic factor that varies directly and simultaneously with the business cycle, thus indicating the current state of the economy. Examples include nonagricultural employment, personal income, and industrial production. *See also* lagging indicator; leading indicator

collateralized mortgage obligation (CMO)   A mortgage-backed corporate security; unlike pass-through obligations issued by FNMA and GNMA, its yield is not guaranteed and it does not have the backing of the federal government. These issues attempt to return interest and principal at a predetermined rate. *See also* tranche

commercial paper   An unsecured, short-term promissory note issued by a corporation for financing accounts receivable and inventories. It is usually issued at a discount reflecting prevailing market interest rates. Maturities range up to 270 days.

common stock A security that represents ownership in a corporation. Holders of common stock exercise control by electing a board of directors and voting on corporate policy. *See also* equity

constant dollar plan A defensive investment strategy in which the total sum of money invested is kept constant, regardless of any price fluctuation in the portfolio. As a result, the investor sells when the market is high and buys when it is low.

constant ratio plan An investment strategy in which the investor maintains an appropriate ratio of debt to equity securities by making purchases and sales to maintain the desired balance

convertible bond A debt security, usually in the form of a debenture, that can be exchanged for equity securities of the issuing corporation at specified prices or rates. *See also* debenture

corporate bond A debt security issued by a corporation. A corporate bond typically has a par value of $1,000, is taxable, has a term maturity, and is traded on a major exchange.

cost basis The price paid for an asset, including any commissions or fees, used to calculate capital gains or losses when the asset is sold.

cost-push Increasing costs of production, including raw materials and wages, that are believed to result in inflation. *See also* demand-pull

coupon yield *See* nominal yield

current yield The annual rate of return on a security, calculated by dividing the interest or dividends paid by the security's current market price. *See also* bond yield

debenture A debt obligation backed by the general credit of the issuing corporation. *See also* secured bond

debt security A security representing a loan by an investor to an issuer such as a corporation, municipality, the federal government, or a federal agency. In return for the loan, the issuer promises to repay the debt on a specified date and to pay interest. *See also* equity security

default The failure to pay interest or principal promptly when due

demand-pull An excessive money supply that increases the demand for a limited supply of goods that is believed to result in inflation. *See also* cost-push

discount bond A bond that sells at a lower price than its face value. *See also* par value; premium bond

discount rate The interest rate charged by the 12 Federal Reserve Banks for short-term loans made to member banks

dividend A distribution of the earnings of a corporation. Dividends may be in the form of cash, stock, or property. All dividends must be declared by the board of directors. *See also* cash dividend; dividend yield; property dividend

dividend yield The annual rate of return on a common or preferred stock investment. The yield is calculated by dividing the annual dividend by the purchase price of the stock. *See also* current yield; dividend

dollar cost averaging A system of buying mutual fund shares in fixed dollar amounts at regular fixed intervals, regardless of the price of the shares. The investor purchases more shares when prices are low and fewer shares when prices are high, thus lowering the average cost per share over time.

earnings per share (EPS) A corporation's net income available for common stock divided by its number of shares of common stock outstanding.

earnings per share fully diluted A corporation's earnings per share calculated assuming that all convertible securities have been converted.

equity (EQ) The ownership interest of common and preferred shareholders in a corporation. *See also* common stock

equity security A security representing ownership in a corporation or other enterprise. *See also* debt security

Eurobond A long-term debt instrument of a government or corporation that is denominated in the currency of the issuer's country but is issued and sold in a different country.

ex-date The first date on which a security is traded without entitling the buyer to receive distributions previously declared. Also called ex-dividend date.

face value *See* par value

Fannie Mae *See* Federal National Mortgage Association

Federal Home Loan Mortgage Corporation (FHLMC) A publicly traded corporation that promotes the nationwide secondary market in mortgages by issuing mortgage-backed pass-through debt certificates. Also called Freddie Mac.

Federal National Mortgage Association (FNMA) A publicly held corporation that purchases conventional mortgages and mortgages from government agencies, including the Federal Housing Administration, Department of Veterans Affairs, and Farmers Home Administration. Also called Fannie Mae.

fiscal policy The federal tax and spending policies set by Congress or the president. These policies affect tax rates, interest rates, and government spending in an effort to control the economy. *See also* monetary policy

foreign currency Money issued by a country other than the one in which the investor resides.

general obligation bond (GO) A municipal debt issue backed by the full faith, credit, and taxing power of the issuer for payment of interest and principal. *See also* revenue bond

Ginnie Mae *See* Government National Mortgage Association

Government National Mortgage Association (GNMA) A wholly government-owned corporation that issues pass-through mortgage debt certificates backed by the full faith and credit of the U.S. government. Also called Ginnie Mae.

government security A debt obligation of the U.S. government, backed by its full faith, credit, and taxing power, and regarded as having no risk of default. The government issues short-term Treasury bills, medium-term Treasury notes, and long-term Treasury bonds. *See also* agency issue

Investment Company Act of 1940 Congressional legislation that regulates companies that invest and reinvest in securities. The act requires an investment company engaged in interstate commerce to register with the SEC.

lagging indicator A measurable economic factor that changes after the economy has started to follow a particular pattern or trend. Lagging indicators are believed to confirm long-term trends. *See also* coincident indicator; leading indicator

leading indicator A measurable economic factor that changes before the economy starts to follow a particular pattern or trend. Leading indicators are believed to predict changes in the economy. *See also* coincident indicator; lagging indicator

maturity date The date on which a bond's principal is repaid to the investor and interest payments cease.

monetary policy The actions of the Federal Reserve Board that determine the size and rate of growth of the money supply, which in turn affect interest rates. *See also* fiscal policy

money market The securities market that deals in short-term debt. Money market instruments are forms of debt that mature in less than one year and are very liquid.

mortgage bond A debt obligation secured by a property pledge. It represents a lien or mortgage against the issuing corporation's properties and real estate assets.

municipal bond A debt security issued by a state, a municipality, or other subdivision (such as a school, park, sanitary, or other local taxing district) to finance its capital expenditures. Such expenditures might include the construction of highways, public works, or school buildings.

municipal note A short-term municipal security issued in anticipation of funds from another source.

NAV per share The value of a mutual fund share, calculated by dividing the total net asset value of the fund by the number of shares outstanding.

net asset value (NAV)　The value of a mutual fund share calculated once a day, based on the closing market price for each security in the fund's portfolio. It is computed by deducting the fund's liabilities from the total assets of the portfolio and dividing this amount by the number of shares outstanding.

nominal yield　The interest rate stated on the face of a bond that represents the percentage of interest to be paid by the issuer on the face value of the bond. *See also* bond yield

original issue discount (OID)　A corporate or municipal debt security issued at a discount from face value. The bond may or may not pay interest. The discount on a corporate OID bond is taxed as if accrued annually as ordinary income. The discount on a municipal OID bond is exempt from annual taxation; however, the discount is accrued for the purpose of calculating cost basis. *See also* zero-coupon bond

par value　The dollar amount assigned to a security by the issuer. From an equity security, par value is usually a small dollar amount that bears no relationship to the security's market price. For a debt security, par value is the amount repaid to the investor when the bond matures, usually $1,000. Also called face value or stated value. *See also* discount bond; premium bond

pass-through certificate　A security representing an interest in a pool of conventional, VA, Farmers Home Administration, or other agency mortgages. The principal and interest payments are received by the pool and are passed through to the certificate holder. Payments may or may not be guaranteed. *See also* Federal National Mortgage Association; Government National Mortgage Association

point　A measure of a bond's price; $10 or 1 percent of the par value of $1,000. *See also* basis point

premium bond　A bond that sells at a higher price than its face value. *See also* discount bond; par value

prime rate　The interest rate that commercial banks charge their prime or most creditworthy customers, generally large corporations.

realized gain　The amount earned by a taxpayer when an asset is sold. *See also* unrealized gain

revenue bond　A municipal debt issue whose interest and principal are payable only from the specific earnings of an income-producing public project. *See also* general obligation; municipal bond; special revenue bond

secured bond　A debt security backed by identifiable assets set aside as collateral. In the event that the issuer defaults on payment, the bondholders may lay claim to the collateral. *See also* debenture

special revenue bond　A municipal revenue bond issued to finance a specific project. Examples include industrial development bonds, lease rental bonds, special tax bonds, and New Housing Authority bonds. *See also* revenue bond

stated value　*See* par value

stated yield　*See* nominal yield

stripped bond　A debt obligation that has been stripped of its interest coupons by a brokerage firm, repackaged, and sold at a deep discount. It pays no interest but may be redeemed at maturity for the full face value. *See also* zero-coupon bond

Student Loan Marketing Association (SLMA)　A publicly owned corporation that purchases student loans from financial institutions and packages them for sale in the secondary market, thereby increasing the availability of money for educational loans. Also called Sallie Mae.

subordinated debenture　A debt obligation, backed by the general credit of the issuing corporation, that has claims to interest and principal subordinated to ordinary debentures and all other liabilities. *See also* debenture

tax preference item　An element of income that receives favorable tax treatment. The item must be added to taxable income when computing alternative minimum tax. Tax preference items include accelerated depreciation on property, research and development costs, intangible drilling costs, tax-exempt interest on municipal private purpose bonds, and certain incentive stock options. *See also* alternative minimum tax

tranche   One of the classes of securities that form an issue of collateralized mortgage obligations. Each tranche is characterized by its interest rate, average maturity, risk level, and sensitivity to mortgage prepayments. Neither the rate of return nor the maturity date of a CMO tranche is guaranteed. *See also* collateralized mortgage obligation

Treasury bill   A marketable U.S. government debt security with a maturity of less than one year. Treasury bills are issued through a competitive bidding process at a discount from par; there is no fixed interest rate. Also called T-bill.

Treasury bond   A marketable, fixed-interest U.S. government debt security with a maturity of more than ten years. Also called T-bond.

Treasury note   A marketable, fixed-interest U.S. government debt security with a maturity of between one and ten years. Also called T-note.

unrealized gain   The amount by which a security appreciates in value before it is sold. Until it is sold, the investor does not actually possess the proceeds of the sale. *See also* realized gain

unsecured bond   *See* debenture

yield   The rate of return on an investment, usually expressed as an annual percentage rate. *See also* current yield; dividend yield; nominal yield; yield to call; yield to maturity

yield curve   A graphic representation of the actual or projected yields of fixed-income securities in relation to their maturities

yield to call (YTC)   The rate of return on a bond that accounts for the difference between the bonds acquisition cost and its proceeds, including interest income, calculated to the earliest date that the bond may be called by the issuing corporation. *See also* bond yield

yield to maturity (YTM)   The rate of return on a bond that accounts for the difference between the bond's acquisition cost and its maturity proceeds, including interest income. *See also* bond yield

zero-coupon bond   A corporate or municipal debt security traded at a deep discount from face value. The bond pays no interest; rather, it may be redeemed at maturity for its full face value. It may be issued at a discount, or it may be stripped of its coupons and repackaged. *See also* original issue discount bond; stripped bond

Index